Country Walks

in Warwickshire and Worcestershire

Des Wright

Meridian Books

Published 1996 by Meridian Books

ISBN 1-869922-33-6

A catalogue record for this book is available from the British Library

Meridian Books
40 Hadzor Road, Oldbury, Warley, West Midlands B68 9LA

Printed in Great Britain by BPC Wheatons Ltd., Exeter

Contents

Publishers' Note

Every care has been taken in the preparation of this book. All the walks have been independently checked and are believed to be correct at the time of publication. However, no guarantee can be given that they contain no errors or omissions and neither the publishers nor the author can accept responsibility for loss, damage, injury or inconvenience resulting from the use of this book.

Please remember that the countryside is continually changing: hedges and fences may be removed or re-sited; footbridges and river banks may suffer from flood damage; landmarks may disappear; footpaths may be re-routed or ploughed over and not reinstated (as the law requires); concessionary paths may be closed. If you do encounter any such problems the publishers would be very pleased to have details. Obstructions to rights of way should always be reported to the appropriate local authority. These are:

Warwickshire:
Rights of Way Section
Planning and Transportation
  Department
Shire Hall
WARWICK
CV34 4SX

Hereford and Worcester:
Rights of Way Section
County Hall
Spetchley Road
WORCESTER
WR5 2NP

Introduction

WALKING is one of the most popular participatory sports, if not *the* most popular one, in Britain. However, walkers do not need to campaign for new leisure centres, swimming pools, tennis courts and the like. We have inherited our leisure facilities in the form of the vast network of public footpaths which criss-crosses this country. It is very important that these paths remain open and the work done by walkers' groups (from such giants as the Ramblers Association through to the small, local groups with a handful of members) and by local authorities in clearing, waymarking, installing stiles and signposting has helped us enormously. It is my belief that very few walkers seek to trespass or to confront farmers and landowners and the use of waymarks is slowly reducing this problem.

Having lived the first sixteen-or-so years of my life in villages in south Shropshire, my fascination with the English countryside is, perhaps, understandable! There is so much to excite the senses! The smells (how can one describe the unique odour of a horse chestnut 'conker' fresh out of its prickly casing in the autumn?), the sounds (from the song of a spiralling skylark to the sound of a church clock drifting across the meadows), the colours (from the brilliance of a stained-glass window with sun streaming through it, through the tapestry of tints of wild fruits on the hedgerows in late September to the austere black-and-white of hoar frost on bare trees on a sunny February morning) and the peace and tranquillity to be found inside a tiny old country church. Warwickshire and Worcestershire (the latter shortly to be divorced from Herefordshire with which it was unwillingly merged by bureaucrats in 1974!) are very well-endowed with such treasures and I have tried, in the notes scattered within the walk directions, to draw my readers' attention to some of them – for I know that walkers often welcome such snippets of information as they provide an excuse for a brief rest on their journeys!

There are real gems amongst the village churches in the two counties though, sadly, many have to remain locked during the week in an effort to defeat thieves and vandals. There is varied and interesting wildlife – both animals and plants – to which, being an enthusiastic natural historian, I have made reference from time to time. Since most of the walks in this volume are in the north of the region, they do not visit its two major rivers, the Avon and the Severn. However, other, smaller, natural watercourses abound, the Alne, Arrow, Blythe and Salwarpe being attractive examples. Additionally, the area's canals, though man-made, provide fascinating corridors of leisure, often passing through beautiful countryside. Our congratulations are due to British Waterways for the work done in clearing towpaths and encouraging walkers.

My thanks are due to my faithful team of path-checkers which includes Pauline (my wife), Susan (my daughter), Neil Simon (Susan's husband) and our good friends Shirley and Bill Harris. Special thanks go to my son Chris for his carefully-prepared maps. However, these should be supplemented, where possible, by Ordnance Survey maps, the Pathfinder series being of particular value to walkers since it provides extra details such as field-boundaries. Finally, I am most grateful to my publisher Peter Groves for his photographs, for his route-checking – he has checked every walk personally! – and for his advice and encouragement during the preparation of this book.

One of the joys of walking is seeing people of all ages, as individuals, as families and in larger parties, enjoying this healthy sport, all operating at whatever pace they choose. With the young and the not-so-young in mind, the walks included vary in length from 2½ to 8½ miles (though walks 1 & 3 and 16 & 17 may be combined to provide longer excursions). Most of them are on the flat, there being very few steep climbs. For years, I have enjoyed walking them and I hope that I can help you to enjoy them too! I may meet you on one or more of them – I will recognise the book in your hand!

Good walking!

Des Wright
Kings Heath, Birmingham

Using this book

A LL the walks are circular, delivering you back to your car or, in most cases, to public transport. Where public transport is known to be available, brief details are given in the introductory box to each walk. However, changes are not uncommon so for up-to-date information and for news of new services and of old ones which have been withdrawn you should contact:

British Rail	0345-484950
Centro (West Midlands)	0121-200 2700
Warwickshire Transport Operations	01926-412135
Hereford and Worcester County Busline	01345-125436

The location of suitable car parks is given wherever possible; otherwise roadside parking is necessary. Where pub car parks are mentioned, landlords have been consulted. However, ownership may have changed so it would be courteous to ask their permission first and to make use of their refreshment facilities later.

At certain times of the year, mud abounds in the countryside and so boots or strong shoes are strongly recommended. Inevitably, parts of these walks are on public roads, some of them narrow. Please be careful! Also, if your dog is keen to enjoy a country walk with you, please ensure that it is kept under control and remember that not every walker is a dog-lover, many being terrified by the over-enthusiastic approaches of some of our canine friends! Several of the walks pass through sheep pastures and, in these circumstances, dogs must always be kept on a lead.

The sketch maps accompanying each walk are intended to serve as guidance and not as replacements for the appropriate Ordnance Survey maps. Even though you may not always need to use them OS maps are invaluable if in emergency, bad weather or other reason you wish to cut short or re-route your walk. The appropriate numbers of the Landranger (1:50,000) and Pathfinder (1:25,000, with much greater detail) are given in the introduction box at the start of each walk, where you will also find grid references (GR) for the starting and finishing points, together with other useful information. (If you are unsure about the grid reference system you will find this explained on the Ordnance Survey Landranger maps.)

It is always wise to carry a compass, a basic first aid kit and some food and drink. Secateurs can sometimes be useful.

Location Map

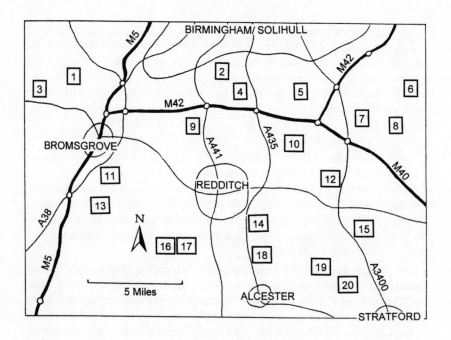

1

A Meander from Pepper Wood

A pleasant country walk which passes through two woodlands (one, Pepper Wood, run on commercial lines by the Woodland Trust) and has good views of the distant Malverns. This walk can readily be combined with Walk 3.

Parking: Car park of Pepper Wood on Dordale Road, near Fairfield, Bromsgrove. (GR938744)
Maps: Landranger 139; Pathfinder 953.
Public Transport: Midland Red West services 318/319 (Bromsgrove – Stourbridge) stop at Wood Lane, Fairfield. From the bus stop, walk up Wood Lane for about a quarter of a mile to enter the main route walk at ✳ on page 4.
Start/Finish: Pepper Wood (GR938744).
Refreshments: The Nailer's Arms and the New Inn (both in Dordale Road, Bournheath) and The Swan Inn (Fairfield).
Distance: 5 miles.
Extended Walk: This walk can be combined with Walk 3 to give a total distance of 11 miles. For details see the box on page 3.

L EAVE the car park, cross Dordale Road and walk up the bridleway (signposted to Royal Content Farm) nearly opposite. Passing barn conversions, walk to the right of the rebuilt Royal Content Farm.

The 'Royal' part relates to the fact that Charles II, fleeing this way after his defeat at the Battle of Worcester in 1651, may have rested here; the 'Content' part of the name presumably refers to his being satisfied with his accommodation!

Continue, with hedges to the left, through four fields with the Malverns visible ahead on clear days. On reaching Warbage Lane turn right and, in 15 yards, go left into Woodland Road. 30 yards after passing Church Road, take a right turn between houses to walk down an enclosed pathway. After descending steps and crossing a footbridge, turn left and, in just over 100 yards, swing right and walk up an incline between mature woodland to the left and a plantation of young oak and ash trees on the right.

At the top, cross a stile and go ahead through two paddocks, passing a pool. At the end of the second of these, climb a stile which admits you to another wood. Immediately crossing two plank bridges, soon veer right,

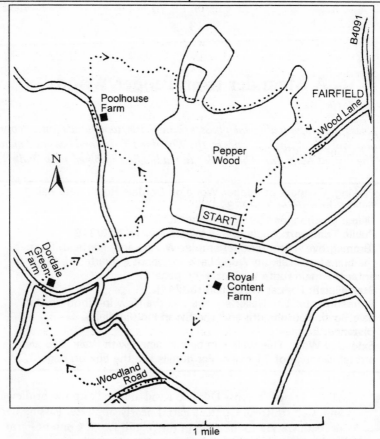

1 mile

ignoring a thin path to the left, to follow a wandering, but fairly clear, path for about 300 yards. On leaving the wood via a stile, cross another paddock to a stile almost opposite and come to Dordale Road again.

If you are doing the combined walk this is where you start your return to Chaddesley Corbett. Now continue reading from ◉ in the box on page 3

Turn left and, immediately beyond Dordale Green Farm with a huntsman-and-hound weather vane on its barn, take a signed path to the right.

❂ *Join the walk here if you are combining it with Walk 3.*

Soon passing through two metal farm-gates, with an ornamental pool to your right, go slightly right to a stile at the top of the incline. Staying on more-or-less the same heading, walk for just over 250 yards through two fields, with a fence on the right, to a stile leading to a lane. Here turn left and, in 20 yards, take a stile on the right and pass along the field's left-hand margin.

Bearing left after a grassy bridge, you come to a double stile on your left. Cross this and walk ahead, with the hedge at your right hand. At the next stile, walk straight on with the boundary *still on the right* and follow it as it curves round towards a double stile. Beyond this, the path descends to a concrete farm bridge in a dip amongst trees. After passing through the farm gate by the bridge, go quarter-left up the field to a stile from which you turn right into a lane.

Continuing up the lane, take the finger-posted stile on the right about 100 yards past Poolhouse Farm and walk half left up a field to reach another stile. Beyond this, aim for a gap in the hedge a little to the right of a white-painted house. Pass through this and, with the Clent Hills visible ahead left, follow a cart track up the next field.

Almost at the top of the incline, turn right immediately *before* a large hedge gap. You may pause here and look back to admire, on clear days, the view south-westwards. In 10 yards, a path to the left leads to an orchard

An extended walk of 11 miles

Starting from Chaddesley Corbett follow Walk 3 until, shortly after passing through Chaddesley-Randan Woods, you are referred to this box.

Here turn left and walk with a birch coppice initially on the right, then cross a stile and walk with woods on the left through two fields. Cross a lane and continue on the right edge of the wood, noting some fine views to your right.

Cross a stile and walk along the driveway of a bungalow ('Randan') to reach another lane (Woodcote Lane). Turn left along this for about half a mile, then at a T-junction turn right along Dordale Road. In about 30 yards take a signed path on the left.

Now continue reading from ✪ on page 2.

◉ Having completed the Pepper Wood/Fairfield walk, on reaching the road turn left to pass Dordale Green Farm, with a huntsman and hound weather vane on its barn, and the path that you took earlier. Reaching the T-junction turn left along Woodcote Lane for about half a mile to reach the driveway of 'Randan' (NB *Not* Randan Cottage which is 200 yards earlier). Turn right along this, cross a stile to the right-hand side of a wooden garage and walk along the left edge of the wood. Cross a lane and go over a stile to walk with the wood on your right through two fields. Cross a stile and turn left to rejoin the Chaddesley Corbett walk at ✶ on page 13.

through which you pass to reach another stile. Crossing this, go left, soon
entering a spinney within which is a pool.

*Trees alongside the path in the spinney support good specimens of
ivy, Hedera helix, a plant rich in mystery and mythology. Although
it is not essential for the plant to climb (it often grows in thick carpets
on woodland floors), when it does so, it benefits from greater exposure
to light. The plant up which it climbs gives mechanical support but
nothing else, the ivy having its own well-developed root system. The
leaves vary greatly in shape, those here being quite sharply pointed,
with conspicuous veins. You will see plenty of other shapes later on
the walk.*

150 yards after the spinney, you reach a hedge gap where you turn left
and embark on a path which arcs round the perimeter of a large field
where, 100 yards after passing beneath electricity lines, you take a
waymarked turn to the left. This leads, via a footbridge, through a narrow
extension of Pepper Wood. Emerging from this, the path goes left for a
little over 15 yards and then veers right beside a fence. After hugging the
edge of the wood at your right side for about 35 yards, pass through
another of its slim arms. Again go left and soon right, cross a stile and then
continue with the wood's edge on the right until, after about 400 yards,
you pass over a stile in a row of oak trees. 75 yards beyond this, the path
goes right and, after another 150 yards, drops abruptly to a footbridge,
continuing up the other side so passing through the third of Pepper Wood's
narrow tendrils.

Leave the wood via a stile on the ground around which are, in autumn,
large numbers of the three-pronged, winged fruits of the hornbeam tree
which is standing 10 yards to the left. Go up a field, with the wood still
on the right, to a stile, cross it and immediately turn left and walk straight
along the boundary of a field to reach a stile.

*If you are using public transport (5 mile walk) turn left after
crossing the stile into Wood Lane and walk down to Fairfield.*

Crossing this, turn right into Wood Lane.

*∗ If you are using public transport join the walk here, continuing
up Wood Lane.*

About 150 yards after Wood Lane Farm, directed by a signpost, turn
left and, ignoring a stile on the left, follow the blue waymarks to enter
Pepper Wood.

*Pepper Wood is owned by The Woodland Trust, founded in 1972
to protect native woodlands in Britain, and is a remnant of the Forest
of Feckenham, also referred to on walks 3 and 13. It covers an area
of 134 acres and, in addition to a wide range of tree species, its
clearings house many wild flowers, bluebells and wood anemones*

being much in evidence in springtime. The tracks of Muntjac deer can sometimes be seen in mud and, in summer, visitors may be fortunate enough to observe the display flight of the woodcock.

Follow the distinct, chippings-surfaced bridleway as it gradually descends for about half a mile through this interesting area, finally reaching your transport in the car park.

If you joined the walk in Wood Lane, or are following the longer walk, cross Dordale Road, as described at the beginning of the text, and continue reading from there.

2

Wast Hills and a Tunnel

Being very close to the southern boundary of Birmingham, this walk provides a handy escape into pleasant countryside with a brief visit to the Worcester and Birmingham Canal.

Parking: Forhill Picnic Place, between Hopwood and Wythall. (GR055755). Before you leave please take note of the time at which the gate is locked. It is displayed by the main gate.
Maps: Landranger 139; Pathfinder 954.
Public Transport: Midland Red West service 146 (Birmingham – Evesham) stops at Ash Lane, Hopwood. If you are starting here walk into Ash Lane which is just south of the petrol station. About 200 yards after a sharp right bend, reach a no through road sign. Here turn left into Stonehouse Lane, joining the main route in another 200 yards. Then start reading from ✱ on page 9.
Start/Finish: Forhill Picnic Place (GR055755).
Refreshments: The Peacock Inn and, for those travelling by bus, Hopwood House Inn.
Distance: 4½ miles.

L EAVING the picnic place via the main gate, turn right into Ryknild Street (a variant spelling of Icknield Street) and immediately left into Lea End Lane with the Peacock Inn on the corner. Opposite the post-box in the wall of the pub, turn right (left if you are using the public transport alternative) directed by the fir-cone waymarks of the 26 mile-long North Worcestershire Path (which runs from Kingsford Country Park, near Kinver – where it joins the Staffordshire Way – to Major's Green, Shirley), to enter an unnamed lane.

After about 400 yards and just before the entrance to the second farm, cross a plank bridge and stile on the right. Then, following the waymark's direction, walk three-quarters left towards the nearest of a line of trees where another waymark directs you round the field margin to your left. Having passed a C-shaped duck pond, negotiate a dog-friendly stile and bear slightly right along a muddy-in-winter cart track towards another stile in the corner of the field.

Hugging the hedges on the right, pass through two fields with views to the Lickey Hills to the left ahead. At the end of the second field, cross the second stile and, passing along a narrow path for 20 yards, turn left onto a roughly-tarmacked track.

The pastoral scene abruptly changes for, on the right, you now have a panoramic view towards the city of Birmingham. You can pick out the clock tower of the University of Birmingham, the Queen Elizabeth Hospital, the Telecom Tower and the Rotunda in the city centre and, nearer the foreground, the tower of St Nicholas' Church, Kings Norton.

Resuming the walk, the track wanders through a spinney, finally sloping downwards to bear right past an ornamental iron gate to reach a stile. Moving straight ahead, on the left boundary of two fields, you finally come to Wast Hills Lane where you go left, parting company with the North Worcestershire Path.

As the lane swings to the left and inclines downwards, turn right over a stile beside a metal farm gate. Walk half left across the field to go through a gate. Then turn left to follow the hedgerow at the end of which, beneath an oak tree, cross another stile. Looking across the large field, you will see the next stile $45°$ to the right, just to the left of a clump of coniferous trees.

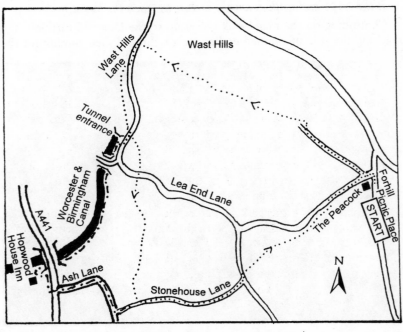

Reaching a lane you will see a stile opposite and will return to it in a few minutes' time.

Meanwhile, make a short diversion by turning right down the lane. Immediately beyond Tunnel House Cottage, turn right onto a path from which a steep but well-constructed staircase made from redundant railway sleepers leads down to the canal towpath and the entrance to Wast Hill Tunnel.

Despite contradictory metric information – the notice by the towpath says the tunnel is 2465 metres long yet that over the tunnel entrance claims 2493 metres – this tunnel, opened on 27 March 1797, is, at 2726 yards, the longest on the Worcester and Birmingham Canal. Notice the lack of a towpath in the tunnel. It would therefore be necessary for the occupants to 'leg it' through the tunnel while the horses were walked over the top to the other end, in Hawkesley.

Having, with luck, seen a boat enter or emerge from the tunnel, retrace your steps up the staircase – 32 of them!.

If you have travelled by bus leave the main walk here. At the top of the staircase, turn sharp right and take a path which gradually leads down to the canal towpath. Walk along this and, on passing under the third bridge, turn left up steps to Hopwood House Inn. Turn right at the A441 and walk down the incline to reach the bus stops.

Continuing on the main walk go on up to the lane and turn left. On reaching the stile mentioned earlier, turn right and then, aiming for the

The entrance to the Wasthill Tunnel

large tree just to the right of the white houses, walk down the field. At the tree, go half right to reach a stile lying between an oak and an ash on a lane – Lea End Lane again!

Long-range weather forecasting these days is based computer-analysed information. Such predictions in the past depended on the signs of nature. 'The oak before the ash, we're going to get a splash; the ash before the oak, we're going to get a soak' depended on comparing the times at which leaves appeared on these two trees. One wonders which method was the more accurate!

Crossing the lane – with caution, there being a blind bend to the right – pass through a farm gate directly opposite. Go straight ahead towards an electricity post in the far left hand corner of the field. Here cross a stile and, following the direction of the waymark, aim half left up the incline to find a gateway in the far corner of the field.

Ignoring an adjacent stile, pass through the gateway and go ahead with the hedge on the left to a stile over which you pass. Instead of going straight ahead, walk slightly to the left to find, at the bottom of a bank opposite, a waymarked stile leading to a footbridge. After crossing this, the path swings left up to a field where, keeping to the left hand margin beside the stream, you reach a stile in a dip alongside holly trees. Beyond this, turn half right to a metal farm gate through which you pass to use a tractor track to Stonehouse Lane into which you turn left.

✶ *If you have travelled by bus join the walk here.*

You soon pass Brookhouse Farm where you might have a touch of vertigo when thinking of those who have to paint the eaves of the tall farmhouse! Stay on this lane for just over half a mile. At a T-junction, turn left into Watery Lane and, in 10 yards, use a stile on the right. This is immediately followed by steps leading to a further stile, one in a series maintained by the Alvechurch Village Society.

Walkers are grateful to members of voluntary groups, from small ones like the Alvechurch Village Society and the Wythall Countryside Carers (mentioned in Walk 4) to the Ramblers' Association with its membership of 100,000+, who put in much time and effort to make walkers' lives more pleasurable and to maintain paths which might otherwise degenerate.

Having crossed this stile, walk up the field alongside a curving strip of woodland at the end of which scale another stile. Then walk straight up the next field for about 170 yards to reach, about half-way up the field, the corner of another field where, after ascending a few steps, climb yet another stile. Following the left hand margin, proceed past ash trees displaying, in winter, their funereal black buds.

At the top of the field, turn left, pass through a gateway and then turn immediately right to resume your former heading. Pass over a further stile and, keeping close to the left-hand hedge, walk up a grassy incline towards trees. Negotiating another stile, enter woodland surrounding a long-deserted quarry. The path wanders between the trees, soon veering left to a lane – Lea End Lane, yet again! Here turn right and, in just over 200 yards, reach your starting point at the picnic site.

If you have travelled by bus now turn left opposite the post box in the wall of the Peacock Inn and continue reading from the second sentence of the first paragraph on page 6.

An invitation at the end of the walk!

3

Around Chaddesley Corbett

This short walk, starting at the imposing Chaddesley Corbett Church, crosses farmland and passes through a woodland nature reserve after which there may be good views of Shropshire's Clee Hills. It can easily be combined with Walk 1 if a longer excursion is required.

Parking: Roadsides near Chaddesley Corbett church. (GR892735).
Maps: Landranger 139; Pathfinder 953.
Public Transport: Midland Red West services 133, 134 and 136 (Bromsgrove – Kidderminster) stop at Chaddesley Corbett.
Start/Finish: Chaddesley Corbett (GR892735).
Refreshments: The Talbot Inn, the Swan Inn and a tea-shop on the main street.
Distance: 3½ miles.
Special Feature: The main street of Chaddesley Corbett has a fascinating variety of buildings which are explained in a handy booklet available in the church.
Extended Walk: This walk can be combined with walk 1 to give a total distance of 11 miles. For details see the box on page 3.

THE first documentary evidence of the existance of Chaddesley Corbett was in AD816. With the busy A448 (Bromsgrove to Kidderminster road) behind you, walk along the pretty main street until, after 400 yards, opposite a black-and-white, timber-framed cottage, turn right into Hemming Way. As this road swings to the right, use a stile on your left (signposted to Bluntington) and, walking down a slope with a paddock fence on your right, reach a footbridge.

Crossing this and going ahead across a vast rhubarb field, you will come to a patch of willows where you swing slightly right to join a tarmacked track. When, after 150 yards, this track veers to the left, carry straight on up a grassy incline with a hedge to your right. 30 yards beyond a double electricity pole and immediately opposite the first trees of a large orchard, take a thin path to your right – a path that is easily overlooked.

This path goes up a short, sharp incline and passes through the line of the hedge and then turns left. Initially with the now-unkempt hedgerow at your left hand, walk onwards, passing in front of a brick-built bungalow,

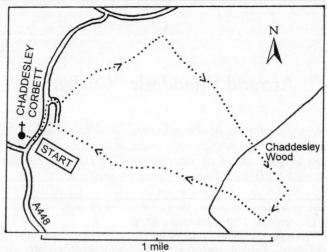

1 mile

to reach a farm lane. Turn right into this lane to reach the farmyard of
Swancote Farm and pass to the right of a red-brick barn which bears a
swan on its weather vane.

Having passed through the farmyard via two gates reach a gate on the
left. N.B. *The Ordnance Survey maps are rather confusing at this point.
The Landranger map shows the path continuing along the cattle track that
you have followed through the farmyard. However, the Pathfinder map
shows that it actually runs parallel to the cattle track on the other side of
a hedge!* So go through the gate and walk with the hedge on your right
(thereby avoiding the cattle track which can be very muddy). The path
swings left at the bottom of the field and, in a few paces, climb a stile taking
care at the other side where there is a nasty drop. Aiming for the farm on
the hillside opposite, walk down the next field at the bottom of which you
find a footbridge. Having crossed this, follow the path which clings to the
left-hand boundaries of two fields as you gradually climb towards
Chaddesley Woods which was designated as a National Nature Reserve in
1973. You enter the Reserve via a stile.

*This woodland, part of a larger block known as the
Chaddesley-Randan Woods, originally formed part of the Forest of
Feckenham (referred to on Walks 1 and 13) which was a royal hunting
area. It is thought to be one of the few remaining parts of the native
woodland which covered this part of Britain from primeval times until
the sixteenth and seventeenth centuries. Now managed by English
Nature (formerly The Nature Conservancy Council), the reserve
contains a wide range of plant and animal species. (Further details are
available from English Nature on 01684-560 616). You will be using*

the Jubilee Walk which was set out in 1977 to mark the 25th anniversary of the Queen's accession to the throne.

In the reserve, a clear path leads up a long, gentle incline. Continue to the brow of the hill and then walk downwards for about 50 yards.

If you are following the longer walk this is the point to leave this one for the time being. Turn now to the box on page 3 for details.

Otherwise turn right...

✳ *Rejoin the walk here if you have been following the longer option.*

... and follow the path between birch scrubland on the left and a conifer plantation initially lined by beech on the right. Ignore a path left and 40 yards after your path merges with the forest road turn right and follow another clear path down a slope.

At the bottom of this slope, the path veers a little to the left (*don't go into the grassy area*) and climbs gently, maintaining more-or-less the same heading. You will be directed from time to time by hand-painted, yellow waymarks on surrounding trees and serenaded, in spring-time, with delightful bird-song. As you emerge from the wood, a very pleasant view confronts you on clear days with Shropshire's Clee Hills in the far distance to the left and right of the tower of Chaddesley Corbett church.

Your next stile lies straight ahead and, beyond it, a well-trodden path leads down to a further stile beside a tree-surrounded pool. The path now follows the line of the hedge as it meanders towards the village, in several hundred yards joining a farm track. Just beyond the now-converted Vicarage Farm, go straight ahead over a stile, leaving the farm track as it swings off to the left. After leaving a market gardener's land, drift slightly right and left and soon rejoin the main street opposite to the Swan Inn. Turn left here and walk for a little over 100 yards to the church.

The church is said to be the only one in England dedicated to Saint Cassian. It is a fine building with twelfth century remnants – Norman pillars and arches on the north side of its nave, a Norman font complete with dragons and a blocked-off Norman north door. The chancel is fourteenth century, but nonetheless impressive. Your visit will be made more meaningful by the useful explanatory literature which is available inside the church.

4

Wythall and a Transport Museum

This is another walk which contrasts the bustle of city life with the rural tranquillity of north Worcestershire which is so near-at-hand.

Parking: Roadside by the church in Chapel Lane, Wythall (GR073749). Also at the Birmingham and Midland Museum of Transport in Severn Way, off Chapel Street for those visiting the Museum (GR072751). (Check time at which gates are closed before leaving!)
Maps: Landranger 139; Pathfinder 954.
Public Transport: The following bus services stop at Wythall Church: 172 and 175 (from Solihull) and Midland Red West 177 (from Birmingham). Also from Birmingham the Midland Red West 178 service stops at Wythall by-pass traffic island. From here walk forward (south), then turn right to cross the A435. Swing right and then turn left along Chapel Lane to reach the church and the Transport Museum.
Start/Finish: Wythall (GR073749).
Refreshments: Coach and Horses public house.
Distance: 4 miles.
Special Feature: Birmingham and Midland Transport Museum. This is open to the public and opening times may be checked by telephoning 01564-826666.

IF you have started from the Transport Museum (the Birmingham and Midland Museum of Transport), walk down Severn Way to join Chapel Lane with the Wythall Church on your right.

The brick-built church of Saint Mary was built in 1862, its splendid tower being added in 1903. The church is no longer used for worship, notices warning those who approach it of the danger of falling masonry.

Immediately beyond the church and its adjoining old schoolroom, turn right and walk down to the end of the farmyard of Chapel Green Farm. Pass through a wide gateway and then aim half-left across a field to another gateway, which is initially out of sight, just to the right of a large clump of trees.

Maintaining the same line, cross another field to a footbridge. Beyond the bridge walk up through two further fields with their margins on your right. Just after a shaded, moorhen-rich pool, pass over a stile by a gateway and then bear abruptly left to a stile which lies on a line just to the right of farm buildings. Across the lane, walk up a farm drive for 20 yards then cross a stile on the right. Walk towards the hedge to the right of the farmhouse garden and then follow the line of this hedge to a lane.

Crossing this, enter a track opposite which passes renovated barns. At the end of this track, climb over a stile alongside a well-constructed finger-post provided by the Wythall Countryside Carers, a local voluntary group. The post is sited at the meeting point of the parishes of Beoley, Alvechurch and Wythall. Following the direction of the pointer to Alvechurch, go half-right through a gap in a wooden fence and continue on the same line to the corner of the field where you cross another stile.

Walking ahead, cross two fields and two stiles. After the second of these, veer half-left to a third one which leads to a lane into which you turn right. On your right you will see an old windmill, now minus its sails. After about 500 yards (and shortly after the intriguingly-named Granny's Cottage), a

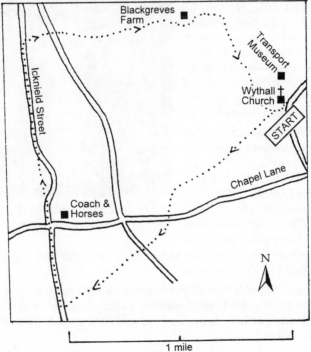

crossroads is reached where, on the opposite corner, is the Coach and Horses. Cross the road, bearing slightly left, to continue on Icknield Street.

Icknield Street is an old Roman road – perhaps a tenth century equivalent of today's Long Distance Paths! As you walk along it, you might imagine yourselves following in the steps of Roman soldiers and horses and stepping over the ruts left by their chariot-wheels.

At the bottom of an incline, just after a bridge, the road swings right but the footpath continues on the original heading. Ignoring the gate on the left, pass around an earth barrier and walk straight up the field. To the left is an enclosed track – could this have been the original line of Icknield Street?

At the top of the incline, cross a stile and, continuing forward, soon find your way back to the unevenly-tarmacked road, having, as the Romans did, walked in a more-or-less straight line. Then follow the road, very muddy in one place in winter,

Finger Post provided by Wythall Countryside Carers

for about half a mile, passing Mount Pleasant Farm and a red-bricked house called The Oaks *en route*.

Just over 150 yards beyond this house, look out, on your right, for two holly trees a few yards beyond which is a stile. Cross this and walk, with the hedge on your left, through a field and then a small copse to a road 200 yards ahead.

Cross this road to a signpost and, 10 yards beyond it, climb a waymarked stile, now joining the North Worcestershire Path. This goes half right across the field to a hedge corner just beyond which is an open gateway. Hugging the left-hand boundary of two fields, the tower of Wythall Church being visible ahead and to your right, your next objective is the white farmhouse ahead. On reaching the moated Blackgreves Farm, your path veers slightly to the right to cross a footbridge and stile. Climb the next stile, just to the right of a bullrush bed, and walk on alongside the moat.

Using the stile ahead of you (not the one taking the NWP off to the left), enter Kings Norton Golf Course via a plank bridge. Immediately turn left and begin to walk round the perimeter of the course on a path diverted in 1990, the original direction still being shown on pre-1990 maps. Just beyond one of the greens, the grassy path passes between hedges and then through a small coppice for about 70 yards before swinging right through scrubland.

About 30 yards before a tall, wire fence, the path veers right to the corner of that fence. Beyond this is Wythall Green, a pleasantly landscaped office campus being developed by Brittanic Assurance. The path follows the fence and, about 30 yards before its end, swings right and crosses a fairway to a stile just to the right of an uneven row of Cupressus trees.

Leaving the golf course via this stile, follow the left-hand margin of fields with mobile homes adjacent, negotiating several twists and turns. Eventually you reach the familiar track which leads you up through the farmyard of Chapel Green Farm. Proceeding with the church to the left, Chapel Lane is soon reached and, by turning left, your transport, whether public or private, is soon reached.

If you have used the car park of the Transport Museum, you owe that organisation a visit and a little financial support.

The Birmingham and Midland Museum of Transport houses a wide range of public transport vehicles. There are buses, railway coaches, a Frankfurt tramcar and electric-powered vehicles such as milk floats, some in running order but others in need of, and receiving, tender, loving care.

5

Earlswood – Woods and Lakes

Another walk within easy reach of south Birmingham and which passes through a pleasant woodland nature reserve and visits Earlswood Lakes with their varied leisure facilities.

Parking: The car park at Earlswood Station is for rail-users only, but there is roadside parking nearby in Rumbush Lane (GR095744).
Maps: Landranger 139; Pathfinder 954.
Public Transport: Trains between Birmingham and Stratford-upon-Avon stop at Earlswood Station. (N.B. This is not the same as The Lakes Halt.)
Start/Finish: Earlswood Station (GR095744).
Refreshments: The Red Lion Inn, Earlswood.
Distance: 4 miles.

LEAVE Earlswood Station via Station Drive and bear right into Rumbush Lane. After 40 yards or so, turn right into a footpath beside which is a watery moat now protecting nothing at all. The path is initially enclosed but opens out a little over 100 yards before a stile leading into Little Clowes Wood, part of the Clowes Wood Nature Reserve. Cross this stile to enter the reserve.

Clowes Wood Nature Reserve has been owned and managed by the Warwickshire Wildlife Trust since 1974. For a reserve so close to the city, it contains a wide diversity of habitats and species, further details of which may be obtained from the Trust on 01203-302 912.

In about five yards, bear right and, in another ten yards, go even further to the right. For about 70 yards, the path follows the wood's boundary. It then swings half left between two fallen trees. 40 yards on, in a clearing, look for a beech tree with, directly behind it, the twin trunks of an oak seemingly in its close embrace. Here turn left and walk down an incline through a beech wood to reach a wooden footbridge. On crossing this, you leave the Nature Reserve and enter New Fallings Coppice which is owned by the Bournville Trust.

Bearing slightly left, walk up the other side to reach, after nearly 200 yards, a concrete marker post which stands between two oaks and which, before it was vandalised, bore information about a nature trail. (This post lies a short distance before a stile leading to a small car park, busy at weekends.)

At the marker post, turn very sharply right and then, in 20 yards, bear left to follow (ignoring branches right) a well-trodden path which runs parallel to, but 40 to 50 yards within, the north-east boundary of the wood. Having passed many holly bushes, you will see, on your left after some 300 yards or so, the Log Cabin belonging to the National Association of Boys' Clubs. (Do not confuse this with a small sports pavilion in the adjoining field.) Turn left and pass to the left of the Log Cabin to reach its main driveway. Follow this until you reach Wood Lane into which you turn right.

On your right-hand side as you turn into Wood Lane is a fine old yew tree. Though old, it is a mere seedling compared with the 5000-year-old specimen which stands in a churchyard at Llangernyw, near Colwyn Bay in North Wales!

Walk on, with care, for about 600 yards until you reach a footpath leading off to the right. This is about 30 yards after a tarmacked drive marked 'Slow, Ramps ahead' and just before No.147 Wood Lane. (If you are in need of refreshment, the Red Lion public house is 500 yards further down the lane.) Follow the footpath until you reach a lake, Engine Pool, where you turn right and pass the foundations of a now-derelict boathouse. You soon cross a stout metal footbridge which leads to a causeway between Engine Pool and, on your right, Terry's Pool.

The three Earlswood Lakes were originally built to feed water into the Stratford-upon-Avon Canal. A wide variety of water fowl is to be

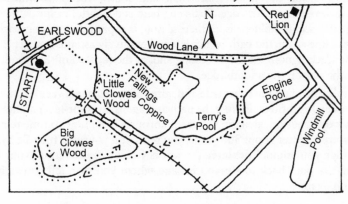

1 mile

*seen including mallards, tufted ducks, common pochard, Canada
geese and great crested grebes – some resident, others seasonal visitors.
Anglers are attracted here and the third lake, which we do not see on
this walk, is called Windmill Pool and is used by a sailing club.*

At the end of the causeway, turn right, ignoring the path and footbridge
ahead, and walk on with Terry's Pool to your right. Note the line of trees
in the pool – marking a field boundary before the area was made into a
reservoir. Towards the end of the pool, the path becomes enclosed with
thorny bushes and then passes between sturdy gate posts. Just beyond
them, turn left and cross a footbridge and two stiles. Walk on forward,
soon passing through an arm of trees extending from a large patch of alder
trees thriving in the marshy conditions on your right.

At the railway embankment, cross a stile and use the path slanting up to
the left to reach the track. Take the advice on a notice – 'Stop, Look, Listen'
and 'Beware of Trains' – before you cross to the other side where another
path slants down to the right. Cross a stile at the bottom and walk across the
field to a pair of stiles connected by a footbridge. Climb over these and walk
on with the hedge at your left hand.

60 yards from the end of the field, the path swings half right to another
pair of stiles in the right-hand corner of the field which you cross. Walk
ahead, the path following the meanders of the stream on your right and
crossing further stiles (one of which seems to be redundant in its isolation!).
When the woodland beyond the stream comes to an end, take the stile on
your right (an awkward one this, like its predecessor, ·designed for tall
people and those not frightened of heights!) and walk up the field with
the woodland still on your right. At the top of the field, use the first stile
to re-enter the Nature Reserve. You are now in Big Clowes Wood.

Once inside the wood, turn right and follow the path which runs
anticlockwise round its edge. Bird-song here is delightful in springtime and
the heady scent of bluebells, in their season, is superb. As you approach the
railway line again, the path swings left and gradually ascends as it gets closer
to the track. Ignore the level crossing and, at the top end of the wood, pass
over the railway via a footbridge.

Walk ahead on the other side and, after 30 yards or so, veer left to cross
a wooden footbridge. Follow the path as it keeps more-or-less parallel with
the wood's margin, swinging inwards abruptly from time to time to avoid
fallen trees. After about 300 yards, you reach, on your left, the stile by way
of which you originally entered the wood. Cross this and retrace your steps
along the path back to Rumbush Lane where you turn left to reach the
station again.

6

Barston and the Knights of Temple Balsall

Starting at Temple Balsall this circuit crosses the River Blythe twice, pays a brief visit to Barston and, back in Temple Balsall, gives an opportunity to explore a truly fascinating church that is steeped in history.

> **Parking:** A car park 'for the use of visitors to Temple Balsall' is opposite the school on Fen End Road, Temple Balsall near its junction with the B4101 (GR208761).
> **Maps:** Landranger 139; Pathfinder 955.
> **Public transport:** Bus 197 from Solihull (Limited service. Phone Centro for times).
> **Start/Finish:** Temple Balsall (GR208761).
> **Refreshments:** The Bull at Barston; Teas (summer weekends) at Temple Balsall almshouses.
> **Distance:** 4 miles.
>
> **!** Wellies probably necessary in wet periods.

LEAVING the car park, turn right and walk down Fen End Road to its junction with the B4101. Turn right into this busy, unpavemented road. Having walked, with caution, along its narrow grass verge for 150 yards or so, turn left into a rough lane, soon using a metal bridge to cross the River Blythe adjacent to a ford. Ignoring an inviting farm gate soon after the bridge, continue along the lane as it narrows into a well-trodden footpath.

In winter, the first 50 yards or so can be very muddy and, further on, there may be local flooding.

When the path meets a tarmacked road, turn right and walk along the road to the first road junction opposite which, adjacent to the metal gates of Barston Park, you climb over a stile. Following the waymark's direction, go three-quarters right across the field to find, a little over 100 yards beyond an electricity post, a double stile. Having crossed this, walk straight across the field to another stile, this in line with a red-brick house.

Having negotiated this stile, turn immediately left and walk 50 yards to go through a gate. You now continue, in the same direction, on a private driveway where, in 80 yards, you use a stile on your right to enter a paddock which you cross to a stile opposite. Climb over this and another, 40 yards later, and then turn sharp right to walk beside a wooden fence at your right-hand side.

At the field corner, turn left to walk up the field in the shade of a tall, hawthorn-dominated hedge. At the top of the field, near to a farm building, cross a stile and, passing along a short, overhung path, enter the churchyard of Barston church.

The church, built in 1721, is dedicated to St Swithin who was Bishop of Winchester and died in 892. Legend has it that, in accordance with his wishes, he was buried in the Cathedral churchyard so that 'the sweet rain of heaven might fall upon his grave'. On his canonization, the monks decided that, to honour his memory, his remains should be moved into the Cathedral. They fixed July 15th for the ceremony. It rained heavily that day – and for the next thirty-nine as well! So they abandoned the idea of exhumation. Hence:

> St Swithin's Day, if ye do rain,
> For forty days it will remain.
> St Swithin's Day of ye be fair,
> For forty days 'twill rain no more.

You entered the churchyard at its south-west corner and walked up a path to the church's west end. You leave at the south-east corner so you need to walk along the south side of the church (with the building at your left hand) and aim for the far right-hand corner. (If refreshments are needed, the public house is on the roadway to the north of the church.) Cross the stile and, following its waymark, go half left through a paddock aiming for a stile halfway along the hedge which faces you. (There is another stile 40 yards further to the left, so make sure that you choose the correct one!) Having crossed the stile, immediately pass through a gap in the hedge and walk southwards down a large field with the hedge at your right.

At the bottom of the incline, pass through as wide gap in the hedge ahead and then follow a path which goes half-left across the field to reach a footbridge. Use this to cross the River Blythe again. Descending the brick steps on the far side, turn right and walk along the field boundary which meanders alongside the river accompanied, on warm summer days, by its attendant damsel- and dragonflies.

These delicate assassins of the insect world live entirely on other insects which they catch in flight aided by their speed, manoeuvrability and acute eyesight. One observer found, in the early part of the century, over a hundred mosquitoes in the mouth of a single dragonfly! However, resting assured that they do not attack humans, you may pause to admire their metallic colours and their aviation skills!

At the end of the field, turn away from the Blythe and, ignoring a plank bridge and stile, follow the field boundary which starts as a wire fence and soon becomes a hawthorn hedge. After about 400 yards, you reach a stile beside a farm gate. Cross this and turn left to walk up the nearside grass verge of Balsall Street for about 80 yards. Here you carefully cross the road to a signposted stile which is slightly obscured amongst trees. Having climbed over this stile, ascend a slight incline at the left-hand side of this large field.

At the top, cross a stile (or go through a gap where there was a stile!) and turn right, ignoring a stile leading in the opposite direction. Now walk in an arrow-straight line for 700 yards with the hedge at your right hand. Turn right into Fen End Road and walk on for about 100 yards where you take a left-hand turn down a farm lane. Follow this lane as it swings right and passes large barns.

Just before the garden wall of the farmhouse, cross a stile on the left, beside a wooden gate, and walk along what might be called a cattle-highway! Though not so bad in winter, when the cattle are confined to the farmyard, this can be very muddy at other times of the year, especially after heavy rain. After about 150 yards, and near water containers, cross a stile left of a gate and turn right onto a grassy path which ends at a wicket gate. Go through this and turn right onto a tarmacked path which leads to a most peaceful spot!

The red-sandstone Church of St Mary the Virgin, Temple Balsall has a long and distinguished history stretching back at least to the fourteenth century, the Knights Templar having been associated with the area for two centuries before that. The church lost its roof and its valuables to Henry VIII's commissioners in 1541 and it lay derelict for many years. The building that you see today is largely the result of a restoration carried out by the famous Victorian architect, George Gilbert White, in the 1840s. There are so many fascinating things to see – its stepped nave, its so-contrasted east and west windows, its altar kneeler containing an estimated 850,000 stitches, its scratch sundials outside the Dames' Door and the large number of carvings of human heads and animals at roof level outside. That's why you are ending your walk here rather than visiting Temple Balsall first!

When you finally tear yourself away from this fascinating building, retrace your steps to the main pathway in front of the church and turn left, soon passing the adjacent Almshouses which were founded in 1674 via the will of Lady Katherine Leveson. At summer weekends teas and ice-creams are available in the old schoolroom here. At the end of the path, you reach Fen End Road into which you turn left to reach the car park.

7

Two Canals and Packwood House

Field paths and the towpaths of two canals are used on this walk and the approach to Packwood House via a splendid avenue of mature trees is spectacular with, in spring, an abundance of daffodils.

Maps: Landranger 139; Pathfinder 954.
Car Parking: Car park and picnic area, Kingswood Junction (GR186710).
Public Transport: Some trains between Birmingham and Leamington Spa stop at Lapworth Station. If travelling by train, on leaving the station turn right into Station Lane and then turn right again at the T-junction at Old Warwick Road. Go under the railway and over the canal, then turn left to reach the car park and picnic area at Kingswood Junction.
Start/Finish: Kingswood Junction (GR186710).
Refreshments: The Boot Inn and the Navigation Inn.
Distance: 6 miles.
Special Feature: Packwood House (National Trust). It is open to the public and opening times may be checked by telephoning 01564-782024.

FROM the Kingswood picnic area join the Stratford-upon-Avon Canal at Kingswood Junction, lock 19. Turn left over bridge number 36 and, in a few yards, just beyond lock 20, walk over a newly-built footbridge and turn left to reach another towpath leading towards the Grand Union Canal.

Rebuilding work, completed in 1996, reinstates a small length of canal, built in 1802 to connect the Stratford Canal with the former Warwick and Birmingham Canal, which is now part of the Grand Union network. Due to disagreements between the two canal companies, in 1812 the link was filled in, boats having to pass through locks 20 and 21 instead of using the 'short cut', thereby wasting two locksful of water (about 50,000 gallons per passage) in addition to precious time and effort!

After passing under a metal, railway bridge, reach bridge 37 which you cross to begin a northerly walk up the Grand Union Canal. Going under

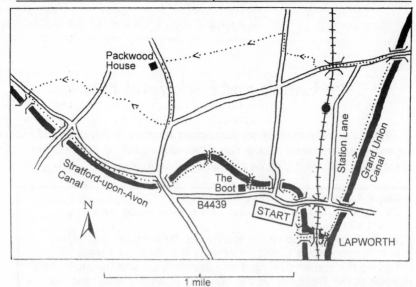

bridge 65, with the Navigation Inn on your right, and occasionally passing the time of day with the occupants of pleasure craft, continue for the best part of a mile in a straight line. In autumn, the hedge by the towpath is brightly decorated with a range of coloured fruits from the blues of elderberry and sloe to the reds of rosehips, haws and white bryony.

You are now on The Grand Union Canal Walk which links London with Birmingham. This 145 mile trek passes by 150 locks and over three notable aqueducts. For those walkers who prefer to walk on the level, this must be near-perfect! Full details may be obtained from British Waterways on 01564-784634.

Immediately before bridge 66, turn your back on the Grand Union and, taking a path to the left, reach a roadway into which you turn left. Follow the road straight ahead as it passes Station Lane on the left and climbs up over a railway bridge. Immediately after the bridge, turn right into a private road which accommodates the public footpath. Just before the house at the end of this road, a waymark directs you to the right. The path skirts around the garden of the house, passing through a waymarked kissing gate *en route*. A second kissing gate leads into another private lane where opposite and a little to the right you pass through yet another kissing gate.

Keeping the hedge on your left, walk up the field to reach a roadway into which turn right. Having walked for about 150 yards, cross a stile on the left to enter Packwood Avenue composed mainly of oaks and limes, with any gaps having been filled with well-protected replacements. Proceed, straight as an arrow, to a pair of stiles between two pools. Having crossed these, continue along the avenue – the oaks gradually giving way to horse chestnuts – to catch your first sight of Packwood House ahead. Leave the park, via a metal wicket gate and steep, brick-built steps, and turn left into a road.

Packwood House is a timber-framed Tudor house, built in about 1550 and containing, amongst other treasures, collections of needlework and tapestry. It also features a renowned yew tree garden, begun in 1650, which represents the Sermon on the Mount. In springtime, daffodils on its roadsides attract many sight-seers. For opening times, telephone 01564-782024.

This road can be busy at weekends in the daffodil season. Follow it for about 600 yards to reach a road junction at which turn right and immediately climb wooden steps to cross a stile. Keeping close to a pool and woodland, pass to the right of a house and walk down a meadow to another stile at the end of the meadow. Cross this and, bearing a little to the left, find a sleepered path which leads over a few yards of wet ground to another stile. Having passed over this, turn right and follow the field margin.

At a waymarked fence stile, leave this field to walk on the edge of Packwood Park with, on your right beyond the pool, good views of the house. Further waymarks lead through tree-studded parkland to a stile which leads into a lane. Cross the lane to walk up the driveway of

Kingswood Junction

Malthouse Farm. Just before its metal gateposts, turn left and walk on with the hedge on your right soon to reach a stile which you cross.

Immediately turning left, walk down a slight incline with the hedge on your left. Having passed a sunken, tree-surrounded pool, the path swings a little to the left to pass through a large gap in the hedge to enter another field along the right hand margin of which you walk. This field narrows and leads to a stile which you cross.

Turn left and walk for about 70 yards on the grass verge of the busy Hockley Heath to Lapworth road. Then cautiously cross the road to a lane which leads to Drawbridge Farm. Just before the lift bridge, turn left onto the towpath of the Stratford Canal to embark on the final, gentle leg of the walk. Cross bridge 30 to use the towpath on the other side, reversing the procedure at bridge 32. As the frequency of locks increases, so the gradient of the slope down which you are walking helps you to free-wheel down to bridge 33 which gives access to The Boot if you are in need of refreshment.

Continue along the towpath passing locks 15 to 18. Walk under a road bridge and, passing reservoirs on your left, return to the starting point of Kingswood Junction.

8

Around and about Baddesley Clinton

This delightful walk encompasses woodland, parkland, field paths and two marvellous country churches with the option of a visit to Baddesley Clinton House.

Parking: Grass verge on Hay Wood Lane, Baddesley Clinton (GR204712) opposite entrance to bridleway to Baddesley Clinton Church. Before parking, check that verges are not too soft!
Maps: Landranger 139; Pathfinder 955 & 976.
Public Transport: Train to Lapworth (adds 2 miles). *See box on the following page.*
Start/Finish: Hay Wood Lane, Baddesley Clinton (GR204712).
Refreshments: 'Case is Altered' public house (no food); Baddesley Clinton House restaurant; Navigation Inn, Lapworth (if using public transport).
Distance: 6½ miles (or 8½ miles if starting from Lapworth station).
Special Feature: Baddesley Clinton House (National Trust). It is open to the public and opening times may be checked by telephoning 01564-783294.

WALK northwards on Hay Wood Lane for about 50 yards and turn right onto a driveway leading to the Old Keepers Lodge. At the top of the drive, enter Hay Wood via a stile. Crossing this, bear slightly right, taking a path which soon widens as it leads you through this delightful mixed woodland, with rusty-barked Scots pine and, in autumn, berry-bearing trees much in evidence.

At an intersection of forest roads, continue ahead on the gently-meandering track until, after 300 to 400 yards, this zig-zags left, right and left more abruptly. In a further 50 yards you will see a waymark on a silver birch tree and this invites you to turn right to a wicket gate through which you pass. Bear half right to a similar gate in the far corner of the field. Having passed through this gate, turn left with farm buildings to your left. Passing through another gate soon bear left to reach Wood Corner Farm.

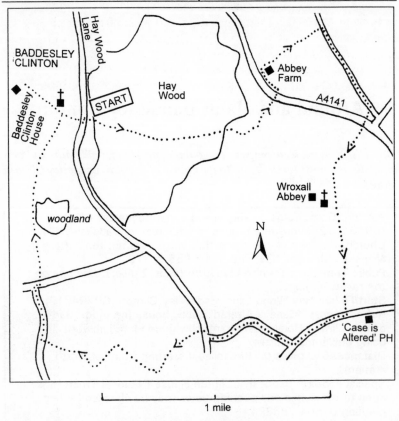

1 mile

Travelling by train

Leave Lapworth station from Platform 1 and turn right along Station Lane. At the T-junction turn left into Old Warwick Road and about 100 yards past the Navigation Inn (possibly a useful stop at the end of your walk) turn left along a waymarked track opposite 'The Manor House'. After about 150 yards cross a stile and then another to the right of a large red-brick barn. Go across the field to the far right corner, passing under power lines.

In the next field walk with a hedge on the right until you cross three stiles in quick succession. Now continue forward on the same heading (NE) until another stile brings you onto the surfaced driveway to Baddesley Clinton Hall. Turn right along this and then, immediately before the gates to the Hall, go left along a signed path to the church. Go through the churchyard, then along a bridleway (E) to the road. This is the spot on Hay Wood Lane where the main walk instructions begin.

In front of the farmhouse turn right into a lane from which you will emerge on a bend on the busy Warwick Road (A4141). Cross with caution and, joining the footpath opposite, turn left. You will soon reach the waymarked entrance to Abbey Farm. At the top of a short driveway, bear left around the barn ahead of you and pass through the farmyard to a waymarked tractor track straight ahead.

The large, honey-coloured cattle to be seen in the vicinity belong to C.H.Evans and Son who specialise in Simmental cattle, their herd numbering about 300 head. This breed was introduced from Switzerland about 25 years ago. Though primarily beef animals, some farmers use Simmentals for production of milk as well as beef. The pedigree stock you will see on this farm is sold mainly for breeding, the herd having produced several champions in major shows in recent years.

Continue to the end of the track and turn right into School Lane which is lined with horse chestnut trees. You will soon pass a tiny cemetery, with its lychgate marked 1898, and houses with elaborate chimney stacks.

Just before the end of the lane, opposite cottages with colourful,

Simmental Cattle

diapered brickwork, take a right turn over a waymarked stile. Now walk through a paddock with Wroxall C. of E. School on your left, noticing a set of wooden stocks which are, we are assured, no longer used on wayward pupils! Having passed through a kissing gate again carefully cross the A4141 to a track opposite signposted to Quarry Lane.

Having passed through two substantial metal gates, you will enter pleasant parkland and, after about a quarter of a mile, follow waymarks to your left passing close to a broad avenue of ancient oaks with its plentiful harvest of acorns evident in autumn. Ahead you will see a fine old, scalloped red-brick wall to the left of which a kissing gate gives you access to a tarmacked road. Continuing on the same heading, passing a duck pond to your left, you will soon reach a main driveway and, looking right, you will see Wroxall Abbey School and a fine old church.

Wroxall Abbey School occupies the present-day red-brick structure built in 1866. An earlier Wroxall Abbey was bought, when he was 80 years old, by Sir Christopher Wren in 1713, soon after Saint Paul's Cathedral had been completed. The church, a fourteenth Century relic of the Priory and dedicated to Saint Leonard, contains several monuments to the Wren family. It is said that the brick wall referred to above was built by Wren, Arthur Mee suggesting that, because of its alcoves, 'some portion of this wall always catches the setting sun'.

Returning to the main drive, resume your former heading, with a wall on your right and a sports field on your left. Pass through a wooden kissing gate in the corner ahead of you and, continuing in the same direction through a sheep field, keeping the fence to your right, reach another stile which you cross. Your next stile, clearly waymarked, is across the field, a little to the right, under an oak tree.

If you need the services of a public house, you may turn left into Case Lane here and, in 50 yards, reach the unusually-named 'Case is Altered' with its pub sign showing two bewigged lawyers studying a brief.

If you have not diverted to the hostelry, turn right into Case Lane, soon gaining a good view of the multi-chimneyed buildings of Wroxall Abbey School across fields to your right. About 100 yards past the last houses, turn right into a lane signposted to Rowington and Chadwick End. Continue along the lane, passing Mousley Hill Farm with its equine weather vane. Down the bank from the farm, bear right at the lane junction.

Very soon after the intersection, you will see a waymarked stile on your left. Cross this and pass along the right-hand edge of a field with, straight ahead, Rowington Church (which we do not visit on this walk). In the right hand corner of the field, cross a stile and plank bridge and turn right. Ahead, you will soon see a stile leading to a metal footbridge. Crossing these and the stile beyond, bear right, following the direction of the waymark, towards a gateway. Just before the gateway, make a 90° turn left, directed by a waymark up to the brow of the incline. (You will have followed a slight dog-leg here, but you will have strictly adhered to the footpaths!)

Cross a stile at the top of the bank and, ignoring its straight-ahead waymark, turn right and follow the hedge on your right. You will soon see ahead of you, towards the left-hand end of a wooden fence, a stile. Cross this and, after a slight zig-zag, pass into a paddock through which waymarked stiles lead you to a lane into which you turn right. Passing Rowington Cricket Club's ground and impressive pavilion, you meet a wider road into which you turn right. In 20 yards, cross to a signposted bridleway and join the Heart of England Way for nearly a mile.

The 80-mile long Heart of England Way is a recognised long-distance path and it links the Staffordshire Way at Cannock Chase with the Cotswold Way at Chipping Campden, passing through Lichfield, Meriden, Henley-in-Arden and Alcester en route.

The blue waymarks of this clearly-delineated track lead you past fields and woodland and, after about half a mile, you will become aware, amongst trees ahead, of the tower of Baddesley Clinton Church. When the bridleway reaches the church driveway, turn left into the churchyard. This is pretty and well-tended throughout the year, but simply idyllic on sunny days when the daffodils and bluebells are in bloom.

The chancel and nave of the Church of Saint Michael date from the fifteenth century, the tower having been added 400 years ago and a screen erected in 1643. There is much to see here but you may also wish to visit the moated, medieval manor house. To do this, you turn right on leaving the church, walk through the churchyard and leave it via a wooden wicket gate. The house, owned by the National Trust since 1980, has changed little since the death in 1633 of the Squire, Henry Ferrers.

If you have come by train now continue past the house and along the lane. Then shortly cross a stile on the left and retrace your steps back to Lapworth.

Otherwise, go back through the churchyard and you will soon reach the driveway of the church. At the end of this you will will see your transport at the opposite side of the lane.

9

Ups and Downs between Alvechurch and Rowney Green

A pleasant stroll up Newbourne Hill for some fine views over the Warwickshire countryside, returning past a venerable eight-trunked oak and through gentle sheep country.

Parking: There is a free car park (GR027727) off Tanyard Lane which branches off Red Lion Street by the Red Lion public house just north of The Square in Alvechurch. To get to The Square from the car park, take either of the paths at the sides of the Baptist Church and then turn right along Red Lion Street.
Maps: Landranger 139; Pathfinder 954.
Public Transport: Midland Red West service 146 (Birmingham – Evesham) serves Alvechurch.
Trains on the Cross-City Rail line from Lichfield to Redditch stop at Alvechurch. If using the train, turn right into Station Road on leaving the station. This leads, via Bear Hill, to The Square which is about half a mile away.
Start/Finish: Alvechurch (GR028726).
Refreshments: The Red Lion and the Centric, both in Alvechurch.
Distance: 4½ miles (5½ miles if travelling by train).

THE walk starts in the centre of the village at The Green. Walk up Bear Hill and, after about 50 yards, take a lane which branches off to the left. On your right as you ascend this driveway, you will see a fine, old timbered building called The Old House. Follow the driveway to reach the churchyard which you enter at its north-east side.

Saint Lawrence's Church stands in a commanding position in the village. It is sandstone-built and has a fifteenth century tower. The firmly-padlocked timber porchway deters friend and foe alike on weekdays but gives sight of a Norman south doorway near to which, in the churchyard, a venerable old yew tree is supported by metal struts. Note the saintly – and the un-saintly – figures on the south wall.

Walk back past the east end of the church and pass through a metal kissing gate in the south-east corner of the churchyard to reach a path which

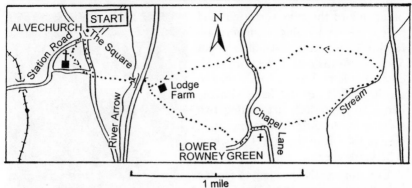

leads to School Lane. Here turn left and walk down to the main road, passing old school buildings. Cross with caution and turn right. In 30 yards or so, turn left into a bridleway towards Lodge Farm.

Follow this until, having crossed the River Arrow, passed beneath a busy motorway feeder road and negotiated a sharp right-left hairpin, you cross a stile on the right to join a well-trodden pathway straight ahead over the brow of a field. Soon pass through a wicket gate and walk on down the incline to pass over a footbridge beyond which your gentle ascent of Newbourne Hill is resumed. Before you enter the woodland towards the top of the hill, take a few moments' rest to look back over Alvechurch village with the Lickey Hills as a backdrop.

Having climbed a short concrete staircase, your path passes through a coniferous plantation. It soon swings to the right, passing between a paddock and a sports ground and later between houses, finally to emerge onto a roadway. Turn left here and walk on until, a little over 50 yards beyond the Rowney Green Peace Memorial Hall, you take a right turn into Chapel Lane. After a hundred yards or so, Chapel Lane swings to the right, but you continue straight on.

If you turn right and follow Chapel Lane, you find, in about 100 yards, Lower Rowney Green Church, a tiny building which is shared by Methodists and Anglicans. This lovingly-maintained, simple place of worship is over a century old.

The track, running due west, is rough-surfaced after leaving Chapel Lane and, at its end, you pass, via two stiles, through a stable yard. After the second stile, continue down the field, swinging slightly left away from the fence, to another stile. Having crossed this, carry straight on for about 80 yards, passing a marshy pool on your left and seeing, to the right, a row of alder trees the buds of which, in some winter lights, provide a Burgundy hue.

After passing over a stream, turn sharply left to cross a stile. On the other side of the stile, turn right and follow the field boundary, ignoring a footbridge which you see after about 50 yards. At the end of the third field, climb a stile and immediately turn to the left. Walk up the field with the hedge on your left, negotiating two stiles *en route*. After the second stile, veer to the left of the gravel pit which is 30 yards ahead.

Continue on this heading to reach a stile between two metal farm gates. Having crossed this and its neighbour, nearly opposite, continue ahead aiming just to the left of trees on the immediate horizon. Cross a stile and,

Grotesque on St Lawrence's Church, Alvechurch

still maintaining the same heading, walk down the field to another stile. Here turn left onto a bridleway and follow it up an incline past a large barn and a white-painted farmhouse at the front of which is a large oak with eight trunks – possibly a result of coppicing many years ago.

On reaching a road, turn right and, in about 150 yards, turn left onto another bridleway. Pass barn conversions on your right and then pass through the farmyard of Alpine Lodge Farm. After an initial portion which can be muddy in winter, the bridleway is stone-chip surfaced for most of its length. After about 700 yards, pass in front of Lodge Farm.

Around the lawns in front of Lodge Farm are to be seen mushroom-shaped stones called 'staddle stones'. These stones would formerly have been used to support a granary and keep it off the ground, so allowing air to circulate and keep the grain dry. The overlap of the stones would also have denied access to rodents like rats and mice.

After Lodge Farm, the path inclines downwards and you soon begin to retrace your steps back towards Alvechurch. On reaching the main road, turn right and walk on along Swan Street for about 500 yards to reach The Square. Alternatively, to avoid the main road, go left up School Lane and return via the church.

10

A Circuit from Tanworth-in-Arden

Starting on the delightful village green at Tanworth-in-Arden, this short walk explores some of the charming countryside of north Warwickshire.

Parking: The Green, Tanworth-in-Arden. GR113705.
Maps: Landranger 139; Pathfinder 954.
Refreshments: The Bell Inn, Tanworth-in-Arden.
Public Transport: Train to Wood End (request stop). Adds 1¾ miles.*See box below for details.*
Start/Finish: Tanworth-in-Arden, GR113705.
Distance: 3½ miles (5¼ miles if travelling by train).
Special Feature: Umberslade Children's Farm. For opening times, telephone 01564-742251.

T HE GREEN at Tanworth-in-Arden is a pleasant spot from which to start your walk. It is dominated by the Parish Church of Saint Mary Magdalene. Well cared for, and with broad aisles and striking stained glass, it is well worth a visit. Its prominent spire will be a useful navigational aid during this walk.

The original Church was built around 1330-1340. Prior to the Reformation in the sixteenth Century, there was probably a

---

Travelling by train

From Wood End railway station take the tarmac path to the main road. Turn left along this to reach the Old Royal Oak pub. Cross the road and opposite the pub go through a gate and along a track which soon becomes a path. Cross a stile into a field and walk forward with a hedge at first on the left. When the hedge swings left continue forward to reach a railway crossing (marked by red warning signs). Cross the line very carefully – trains from the right are coming round a sharp bend.

Entering a field go half left to reach a footbridge to the right of four oaks. Cross this and go straight up the field with a hedge on the right. Cross a stile and now walk with a hedge on the left. After crossing another stile reach the road. Here turn left to walk into Tanworth-in-Arden.

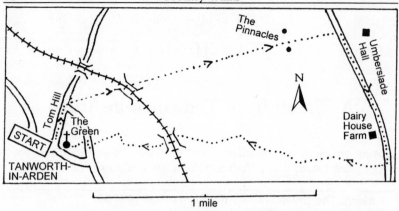

rood-screen across the chancel arch, some of the windows would have
contained stained glass and the walls may have been plastered and
painted with, perhaps, pictures of saints or of biblical scenes. Today's
edifice is based on that fourteenth century pattern, a major renovation
in Victorian times having altered floor levels, installed new roofing
and renovated some of the stained glass.

On leaving the Church by its main (north) door, turn right and walk
down the gently-sloping Tom Hill, passing the village school, with its
unusual arched chimney stack. At the bottom of the bank, take a right turn
following the sign towards 'The Children's Farm' and begin a mile-plus
trek, ruler-straight to the north east. It starts with a metalled road within
a splendid double avenue of mature poplar trees, planted in the late 1950s.

After a hundred yards or so pass under a majestic, three-arched railway
bridge – an extraordinary structure this, faced with a red sandstone and
carrying the Birmingham to Stratford railway line diagonally above us.
About 300 yards past the bridge the road swings right to Umberslade
Childrens' Farm at The Leasowes.

*Frederick Ernest Muntz JP was the owner of Umberslade Hall and
the adjoining estate at the time the Birmingham to Stratford railway
line was being built around 1906. The railway company needed to
gain the permission of Mr Muntz for its new track to cross his land.
After negotiations, he gave his approval provided that the bridge
spanning what is now the avenue should be faced with stone specially
brought from Derbyshire – hence the splendid structure described
above! The Leasowes, a working farm now incorporating the
Umberslade Childrens' Farm, is still run by members of the Muntz
family, one of whom, Mr Fred Muntz, generously provided useful
background information.*

Staying on your original heading, your path now deteriorates significantly being, in winter, very muddy. The regimentation of the avenue trees on your flanks has abruptly been replaced by a disorderly tangle of vegetation with a variety of trees and a rich ground cover in which the red flowers of campion and the white of the cow parsley family are much in evidence in the summer.

At the top of a gentle incline, the vista suddenly widens to reveal, on either side of the path, ornate, stone-built gate-posts, each about 25 feet high. These structures, known locally as The Pinnacles, supported wide wooden gates through which the carriages of the Archer family would drive on their journeys between Umberslade Hall and Tanworth. Continuing until you reach the lane in front of the Hall, you pass horse chestnut trees which, in the absence of foraging livestock, have branches which spread and touch the ground.

Umberslade Hall, built in 1680, was the seat of the Archer family and several tablets in the church in Tanworth commemorate their lives and deaths. The Hall now is subdivided into luxury flats.

Turn right into the lane and soon pass, on the left, the gruesomely-named Hangman's Copse followed by a cottage built on the edge of the moat of the former Codborough Manor House. About 200 yards beyond the timber-framed barn of Dairy House Farm, take a waymarked right turn onto a rough tractor track. Follow this for 100 yards, make a 10 yard deviation to the left, then resume your former heading down a path, keeping a line of trees (the first oak is waymarked), a shady pool and an intermittent hedge on your left.

Having seen St. Mary's spire in the distance, you reach the bottom of the field, turn sharp right and, after just under 100 yards, go left over a plank bridge and stile. Continue ahead with the hedge on your right (ignoring a way-mark which soon invites you to go left), soon passing through a gateway. The hedge at one point swings to the left but still keep it near your right arm until you find that your way ahead is barred by a hedge and fence. Here, go through the metal gate on your right, pass over a brook and bear left through the second (waymarked) gate.

Turn left beside the brook and in about 50 yards reach a waymark post under an oak tree. Here go right, up the field, following the line of two more oaks with the Childrens' Farm now to the right, to reach a prominent stile. Passing over the stile, turn left and proceed under another railway bridge which, by comparison with the first one, is much less salubrious, being brick-built and very damp! Crossing the stile beyond the railway bridge, maintain the same heading and reach a wooden footbridge. Crossing this and keeping the hedge on your left, go through this field up a slight incline and, in spring and summer, maybe hear the yellow-hammer's call, interpreted by some as 'a-little-bit-of-bread-and-no-cheese'.

Whilst recognising the scientific need of Latin names – this one is called Emberiza citrinella – the local names are far more enchanting! The yellow-hammer (or yellow-bunting – 'ammer' is a German word for bunting, so perhaps it should be 'yellow-ammer') is in parts of Shropshire called the 'scribbling lark' because of the brownish or purplish squiggles on its white eggs.

At the top of the field the path veers, with the hedge, 90° to the right. 100 yards after this, using a plank bridge and stile to the left, enter another field. Halfway up this use a stile to switch to the other side of the hedge and continue to the top of the next field. A way-marked stile soon leads to a lane into which you turn to the right and, at a 'School' sign 20 yards on, pass through a metal kissing gate on your left. The path now goes to the left of a large holly tree and skirts the school playing field. A wicket gate gives access to the churchyard and, via the south side of the church, you return to your starting point on The Green.

Returning to Wood End station

Walk back along the road to the footpath by which you arrived, which you will find to the right of 'Little Court'. Cross a stile and walk with a hedge on the right, cross another stile and walk with a hedge on the left, cross a third stile and a footbridge and swing left to carefully cross the railway. Then go diagonally left to meet the hedge and follow this over a stile and along the path to the road, where you turn left, then right to reach the railway station.

11

Avoncroft Museum and Tardebigge

This, a figure-of-eight and the longest walk in the book, starts at an unusual museum, passes a meadow nature reserve, visits two churches of widely-contrasted styles and runs alongside the country's longest flight of canal locks.

Parking: Free parking at the picnic site adjacent to the Avoncroft Museum of Historic Buildings, near Bromsgrove (GR953685)
Maps: Landranger 139 & 150; Pathfinder 974
Public Transport: Midland Red West service 140/141 (Bromsgrove – Droitwich) passes the museum.
Midland Red West service 144 (Birmingham – Worcester): Alight at Stoke Turn which is half a mile from the Museum. Walk about 500 yards along Hanbury Road (B4091) to the Hanbury Turn pub; then go left another 500 yards along Redditch Road and turn right along Buntsford Hill to reach Avoncroft Museum.
Start/Finish: Picnic site adjacent to the Avoncroft Museum of Historic Buildings (GR953685).
Refreshments: The Ewe and Lamb on the B4091; The Queen's Head on the Worcester & Birmingham Canal. Snacks and hot meals at the Avoncroft Museum (open March to November).
Distance: 8½ miles.
Special Feature: Avoncroft Museum of Historic Buildings. This is open to the public and opening times may be checked by telephoning 01527-831886.

O N leaving the picnic site, turn right down the road and, after about 100 yards take a right turn onto a path which is way-marked into and out of the farmyard of Tan House Farm which, in winter, is very muddy. Continue onwards for about 100 yards to cross a stile and then aim for another stile across the field, just to the left of the windmill with the Malvern Hills behind in the distance.

The windmill, a nineteenth-century post mill, is a part of the Avoncroft Museum and was originally sited in Danzey Green, Warwickshire. Since 1976 it has produced stoneground wholemeal flour here and has an unusual cat-and-mouse weather vane.

Follow an enclosed path as it zigzags past first a wild flower pasture and then part of the premises of the Avoncroft Cattle Breeders some of whose prize bulls may be seen beyond its high (and very unwelcoming!) fences.

Until 1990, the Avoncroft Wild-flower Meadow was ordinary arable land, regularly treated with fertilisers and herbicides. At that time, the Worcester-shire Wildlife Trust began an experi-ment there. To eliminate the effect of the added chemi-cals, the top six inches of soil was removed and the field was seeded with a special grass and wildflower mixture. Allowed to revert to the natural state, it is already housing a wide vari-ety of insect and plant life.

The path emerges onto the B4091 road op-posite the Ewe and Lamb public house. Turn left and follow the pavement for about 50 yards and, just past the pub, fork left onto a bridleway which is initially tarmacked and then becomes rougher (and, in winter, wetter!) as it descends a slight incline and swings right over the River Salwarpe. Then ascend a rough lane between houses and emerge into a road, Fish House Lane.

To visit Stoke Prior church, divert right for about 20 yards and pass through a kissing gate in a brick wall. A path then leads to the church which stands in a well-maintained churchyard stocked with numerous yew trees. It has an eight-sided, shingled spire but, like so many country churches, it is generally locked – but more of that anon!

Retrace your steps back to the kissing gate,

Windmill in the Avoncroft Museum

turn left and soon pass the bridleway from which you recently came. Continue along the lane for about half a mile noting, in the hedges in early spring, the abundance of hazel awash with yellow catkins. About 60 yards after Sugarbrook House and a similar distance before the junction with Sugarbrook Lane, take a stile on your right indicated as leading to Copyholt Lane.

Aim for another stile in the far, right-hand corner of this paddock. This leads to a main railway line which you cross with great caution. At the other side, cross another stile and enter an enclosed path which has barbed wire and a thick evergreen hedge on the left. 60 yards past this hedge, cross a stile into the adjoining field, continuing on the same heading with the fence on your left. Aim for another stile which is just in front of canal bridge number 47. Cross this stile, then cross the bridge and, at the end of the brick parapet on your right, duck under a wooden bar and take care as you scramble down a short, steep path to gain access to the towpath of the Worcester and Birmingham Canal.

Although well-used, the route under the wooden bar is not a right of way. A more correct, and easier access is obtained by following the road left to bridge 48 and joining the canal there, opposite the Queen's Head.

Turn right and follow the towpath, passing those who are being refreshed on the terrace of the Queen's Head on the opposite bank. You soon reach the lock 29, Tardebigge Bottom Lock, which is referred to later and is the first step of the Tardebigge Flight, the longest flight of locks in the United Kingdom.

Continue up the towpath until, just before bridge number 52, you turn right dropping down from the canal soon to cross a stile. Then walk across the field to a wooden footbridge, after which you move up an abrupt incline to cross another stile. Aiming a little to the right of the buildings of Patchett's Farm on the brow of an incline, walk to a wide, red farm gate which leads to a bridlepath onto which you turn left. This path is now followed for nearly three-quarters of a mile as it meanders through arable land with good views over Worcestershire to the right.

One of the many reasons advanced for the decline in the number of small birds in Britain is attributed to modern cereal-growing techniques. Whereas in 'the old days' of scything and of cutting and stooking, significant quantities of grain remained amongst the stubble, modern combine harvesters spill very little. Furthermore, today's method of ploughing and re-seeding immediately after the harvest means that any spilt grain is buried and so the winter food supplies for seed-eating birds in the cornfields are almost non-existent.

The bridle path ultimately emerges onto a roadway. Take the lane immediately opposite, High House Lane, and soon become aware of the elegant spire of Tardebigge church ahead. As you near the church, you come to a small group of houses on your left, the last of which is Church Cottage. 50 yards after this, turn left over a stile and, keeping the hedge on your left side, progress up a slight incline. Pass the edge of the school playground to reach a tarmacked path in the churchyard. Here you turn right and, walking in front of the school, soon reach the church. There are several seats hereabouts upon which to rest weary limbs whilst enjoying pleasant views out towards the Clent Hills.

Today's Saint Bartholomew's Church, Tardebigge was built in 1776 as a replacement for its predecessor which was destroyed a year or so earlier when its tower collapsed. At one time, it was bisected by the Warwickshire/Worcestershire county boundary! Arthur Mee described the present building as 'a bright and trim place, looking almost as if it has stepped out of Wren's London'. It is a light, airy building with cushions on some of its pews embroidered with images of narrow boats and lock gates and those of the choir stalls with choirboys and hymn tunes. Having suffered at the hands of arsonists in 1995, the church is, like that at Stoke Prior, kept locked during the week.

On leaving the church, retrace your steps for half a dozen yards and then turn left to walk along the church's south side. Soon after passing an ancient yew, the diameter of the trunk of which is all of six feet, take a kissing gate on the left. You then cross the church car park to a similar gate in the far left-hand corner. Continue ahead on a well-trodden path which curves down the hill to the canal towpath.

Here you may wish to turn right to look at the entrance to Tardebigge Tunnel which is 580 yards long. Having done that, retrace your steps along the towpath to soon reach lock 58, Tardebigge Top Lock.

With a drop of 14 feet, Tardebigge Top Lock is one of the deepest narrow locks in the United Kingdom. When the canal was built there was, at first, a boat lift here. However, such lifts were notoriously unreliable and this one was soon replaced by the present deep lock.

Lock 29, which you passed at the bottom of the flight, was two miles down the hill which means one lock every 120 yards or so – hard work for the canal-users, but the only way of progressing up or down the slope!

Fifteenth Century Merchant's House in the Avoncroft Museum. The first building to be rescued and re-erected in the Museum.

Photo: Avoncroft Museum

As you pass lock 53 you see, on your left, the Tardebigge Reservoir which is the home of such birds as the great crested grebe. This is one of only two reservoirs which feed this canal, the other being Upper Bittell Reservoir. When you reach bridge 52, cross it and climb the stile on the other side and turn left. You hug the field margin until, just after two ivy-covered oaks followed by an ash, you turn left through a field gateway and immediately turn right to resume your former heading, now keeping the hedge on your right. Gradually descend until, having crossed another stile, you join a farm drive which leads to a lane into which you turn right.

Soon reaching a T-junction, turn left and, after 75 yards, leave the main road, passing left into Lower Gambolds, a narrow no-through-road. After about half a mile this swings left to Maidsmere but your footpath continues straight ahead. Carry on and enter a sheep pasture by way of a plank bridge and stile. Keeping the hedge to your right, you reach a gateway where you go straight ahead making for a stile at the far right-hand corner of the field. Using this and a ladder stile on the other side, cautiously cross the railway line and turn left onto a well-defined path which runs parallel to the railway for about 500 yards.

At the end of this path, turn right into Sugarbrook Lane and follow it up a gradual incline. Alertness and single-file walking are essential here and the use, where available, of the intermittent grass verge is recommended. After a little over a quarter of a mile, you see the sign of the picnic site from which you started.

Before you leave, a visit to the Avoncroft Museum of Historic Buildings is recommended. Opened in 1967, over twenty buildings have now been dismantled, carefully restored and re-erected here. The Museum is open from early March to late November.

12

Henley-in-Arden and Preston Bagot

Another varied walk, starting with the bustle of a busy High Street, walking along field paths and a canal towpath and visiting, en route, the delightful church of Preston Bagot with its commanding views.

Parking: Free car park at GR153658. This is reached by going east along the B4095 from its junction with the A3400 at the southern end of Henley and then taking the first turning left. A path from the car park takes you into the High Street where you turn right to reach the Guildhall.
Maps: Landranger 151; Pathfinder 975.
Public Transport: Trains on the Birmingham – Stratford-upon-Avon line stop at Henley-in-Arden. Stratford Blue bus service X20 also connects Birmingham with Stratford-upon-Avon. *If you have arrived by train turn left outside the station and in a few yards turn right along Swan Croft and follow the Heart of England Way signs to reach the High Street. Here turn right for a few yards and cross the road to reach the Guildhall.*
Start/Finish: The Guildhall, Henley-in-Arden (GR151660).
Refreshments: There are abundant facilities in Henley and the walk takes us past the Crabmill public house on the B4095 and the Haven Tea Rooms on the Stratford-upon-Avon Canal.
Distance: 4½ miles.
Special Feature: The High Street, Henley-in-Arden, with its variety of architectural styles, is worthy of attention.

THE walk starts at the fifteenth century Guildhall halfway through the town on the east side of the High Street. Adjacent is St John's Church and you turn into Beaudesert Lane which runs alongside it. At the end of this lane stands St Nicholas' Church.

This church is thought to date from about 1170, though it may be on the site of an earlier Saxon church. The south door, chancel arch and east window are fine examples of Norman architecture. Restorers in 1865 completed the vaulted chancel roof, but where is the pulpit?

Coming out of the churchyard through the oak lych gate, turn left, very soon to reach the lane's end where you ignore the kissing gate but take a well-surfaced cycle path between wooden and concrete fences. Follow this

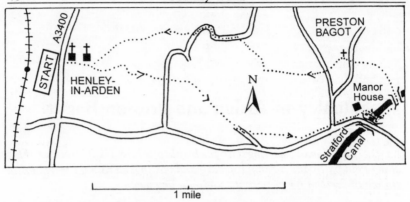

The Norman doorway, Church of St Nicholas, Henley-in-Arden.

path, negotiating at one stage a sharp right-left shuffle and, still keeping to the path, soon pass Henley-in-Arden Junior and Infant School on your right-hand side.

Immediately after the school's playing field the path turns 90° to the right and then twists its way between houses to reach a quiet road. Cross this to enter a path which ends at a wicket gate. Through this, turn half left and start to ascend an escarpment passing a children's play area on your right. At the top of the incline, cross a stile and bear right to another stile ten yards ahead. Having climbed this, turn left and go forward with the hedgerow at your left hand.

The next stile leads into Edge Lane where you turn right for ten yards and then left to pass over another stile. Your next stile, in a wire fence, can be seen ahead and, having crossed it, you walk diagonally across the field to your right to reach a wooden stile halfway along the facing hedge. Having crossed this, continue on the same heading to the far right hand corner of the field where you encounter another stile beyond which is a sunken track.

Almost opposite is a stile. Having negotiated this and maintained the same heading, you reach a gate in the far right hand corner of the field, just to the right of a double electricity pole. Walking through the gate and passing a house on your right, you reach a lane. Here go straight ahead, up the incline. Immediately past the houses on the left, take a left turn over a fence stile and follow the direction of the waymarks.

Keeping to the left-hand hedgerow, walk down a large field at the bottom of which cross a stile and aim across another downward-sloping field to a gate just to the right of the Crabmill public house. Turning left and using the pavement of the B4095 Warwick Road, pass a side-turning to Lowsonford and soon reach the Manor House where you branch left.

The half-timbered Manor House was built in about 1550 to the order of the Earl of Warwick and later became the home of Ingram Bagot. It was extensively renovated in 1975 and, as you pass, you might note its dovecote and the interesting horse-drawn plough on its weather vane.

Leaving the Manor House on the left, soon cross the Stratford-upon-Avon Canal via bridge 47. In a few yards, using a wooden kissing gate on your left, join the towpath at Preston Bagot Bottom Lock. Continuing, and passing one more lock, you reach a bridge which you cross. Now leaving the towpath, go down a bank opposite and, via the edge of a poplar spinney, reach a footbridge by which you cross a stream.

A few yards ahead is a stile. Cross this and walk across the field towards a gateway. We do not go through the gate but, encouraged by waymarks, walk up the field with the hedge on your left.

The Manor House

Some farmers, in the interests of tidiness, slash their hedges in autumn, so depriving birds, particularly those of the thrush family reinforced by migrants from Scandinavia, of their winter rations. This hedge is a picture in the autumn, being richly-laden with colourful hips, haws, blackberries, elderberries and sloes and it must provide a veritable feast for these birds during any harsh winter period.

Pass through an open gateway and, continuing up the slope, go half left from your former heading to reach a stile. Climb this, cross a lane and walk up the driveway and through the car park of All Saints' Church, Preston Bagot. A wicket gate gives access to the churchyard.

Built in the eleventh or twelfth century, the church occupies the site of a settlement set up in Roman and Anglo-Saxon times. Most of the original building still exists today though some of the stained glass has an interesting recent history. This had been removed and stored, prior to the blitz in the 1939-45 war, from a church in Birmingham. That church was destroyed by the bombs, but the glass, now with no home of its own, was later installed at Preston Bagot.

The wooden seat on the south side of the church affords a glorious view over the restful Warwickshire countryside. Leaving the churchyard by the wicket gate opposite its south door, turn to the right to make for a wooden kissing gate in the shade of a fine oak. Go through this to pass an ancient wooden seat carrying the now almost illegible inscription 'Rest and be Thankful'. Having followed a downward path and crossed a lane, pass through a waymarked gate alongside a black-and-white timbered farmhouse.

At the bottom of the meadow cross two waymarked stiles and walk up the next field with the hedge on your right. Crossing another stile, walk up the middle of a field, maintaining the same direction. Your objective is a pair of waymarked stiles, both of which you cross and, in the field after the second stile, hug the right-hand hedge until, just before a house, you turn sharp right. Go through the right hand of two farm gates to emerge into a lane into which you turn left.

In a hundred yards or so, the lane turns right and then begins to curve slowly to the left. 50 yards after a waymarked lane on your right, take a stile on your right and turn half left to walk up the incline roughly following the line of the electricity poles. Reaching a stile at the top of the field, a good view over Henley-in-Arden and beyond is revealed. Having crossed the stile, join a clearly-defined track which swings left down the escarpment and over the Mount.

The Mount is the hill on which, towards the end of the eleventh century, Thurstan de Montford built a Norman castle of wood and stone. The site may well have been occupied much earlier by a British camp. The power of de Montford family was probably instrumental in bringing about the prosperity of the area, a charter being granted by Matilda, daughter of Henry I, for a market to be held in the castle, this attracting much trade.

The slope down from the Mount delivers you down to the end of Beaudesert Lane up which you retrace your steps to the High Street and your transport. For the railway station take Swan Croft by the side of the White Swan.

13

Hanbury Hall

After a brief, steep climb, the views from Hanbury Church are rewarding. The route then passes through woodland, along field paths and a canal towpath, and finally goes through parkland past the imposing Hanbury Hall.

Parking: Roadsides opposite Hanbury School on the road leading up to the Church (GR954642). N.B. The car park by the school is not open to the public and the adjacent lay-by is used by school buses.
Maps: Landranger 150; Pathfinder 974.
Public Transport: Midland Red West service 140/141 (Bromsgrove – Droitwich) – adds 1 mile. Leave the bus at Astwood Lane (GR940656). Walk along Astwood Lane for about 100 yards, cross the canal bridge and turn left to reach the towpath. Go under the bridge (number 41) and walk with the canal on your right, passing the Astwood Locks. Join the main walk just past lock 19. Now start reading from ✳ on page 54
Start/Finish: Hanbury School (GR954642)
Refreshments: Jinney Ring Craft Centre and Restaurant (GR962641); Hanbury Hall (home-made teas are available when it is open). For public transport users, the Boat and Railway, and the Bowling Green at Stoke Works.
Distance: 5 miles, or 6 miles if using public transport.
Special Feature: Hanbury Hall (National Trust). It is open to the public and opening times may be checked by telephoning 01527-821214.

HAVING parked the car you will see that, opposite the school, there is an eroded monument which, on closer inspection, is found to be an ancient Pilgrim Cross which marked an entrance to Feckenham Forest. Facing the school, turn left and, in 10 yards on your left side, find stone steps to a footpath which leads you up a steep grassy incline in the direction of the Church. Enter the churchyard via a metal kissing gate on the south side of the church where seats and redundant pews provide you with a few moments' rest and recovery!

The Parish Church of St Mary the Virgin, built of Bromsgrove sandstone, stands in an commanding position and provides an outstanding panoramic view. There may have been some sort of fort on this hill in Roman times but a thousand years ago a monastery was sited here. The earliest recorded Rector was John de Cernai in 1205. The oldest features of today's church are the pillars in the nave which date from the thirteenth and fourteenth centuries, but most of the building dates from the eighteenth and nineteenth centuries.

On leaving the church by its main (west) door turn sharp right to find, at the north east corner of the churchyard, a waymarked wicket gate. Passing through this, you reach a well-trodden, downwardly-sloping path which leads you, via a two kissing gates, towards wooded Piper's Hill. 80 yards after the second of these and 10 yards beyond a very large oak, move off the main track onto a signposted footpath to your left.

Follow this path for no more than 150 yards along the edge of mixed woodland which includes some ancient, gnarled oaks and patches of beech with bare ground beneath. After those 150 yards, take a thin path to the left *(easily missed and not waymarked at the time of writing)*. If you reach a farm you have missed the path and come twice as far as you should have done!

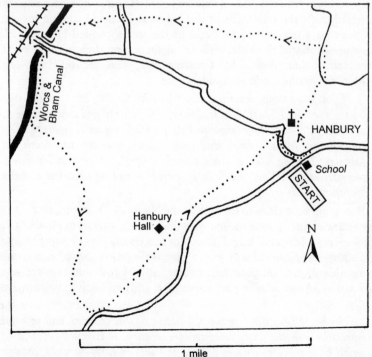

The thin path leads down to a metal hurdle serving as a stile. Your next stile is across the field, 20 yards from its left-hand corner. Keep the margin of the next field to your left and, on reaching its end, cross a plank bridge between two stiles to enter another field. Continue along its right-hand boundary, a thin stream partly obscured by vegetation accompanying you. Using stiles on either side of it, cross a rough farm track and proceed, again using the right-hand edge, through a large field. At a lane, turn right and, in 15 yards, take a stile on your left. Cross this field to another stile which is in line with large oaks opposite.

Proceeding along the left-hand edge of a field, you see, after crossing a footbridge, a stile ahead which leads you to the Worcester and Birmingham Canal.

If you are using public transport now turn right, retrace your steps back to bridge 41, cross it and walk up Astwood Lane to the bus stop. The Boat and Railway pub is to the right, the Bowling Green pub is to the left.

Turn left onto the towpath.

✷ *Start reading here if you are using public transport.*

Proceed past houses, a lock and under a road bridge. At lock 17, Astwood Bottom Lock, take a stile on your left and cross a field to a metal footbridge. At the other side of this, go straight ahead, aiming for a stile by trees on a line just to the right of the tree-shrouded Hanbury Hall. Having negotiated this stile, walk on, again aiming slightly to the right of the Hall, to another stile. Crossing this, you see on your left a double-waymarked stile alongside a gate.

If you have time, you may divert here by turning left over the stile by the National Trust sign. Just over 300 yards ahead amongst trees, you see a 9-foot high monument, part of a pets' cemetery. The monument, built of brick and stone, commemorates the death, on January 23 1857, of a horse called 'Pulpit'. At ground level is a gravestone to 'Allan' – a Scotch terrier? – ending with the epitaph 'Semper fidelis'.

Retracing your steps to the stile by the National Trust sign, cross it, turn left and walk up a gentle incline with the boundary fence of Hanbury Park close on your left-hand side. Follow this fence and, after crossing two stiles and a further pair of stiles by a farm gate, walk on for about 75 yards when you suddenly see, on your left, another stile. Cross this to enter an old orchard by a house. Passing between a pool and a spreading chestnut, reach a stile.

The horse chestnut tree is not a native of this country, having been introduced in the early seventeenth century. It is much-beloved of small boys who frantically collect its fruits in early autumn, though

Hanbury Hall

one rarely sees them play with these at the traditional game of 'conkers'! Incidentally, that name is probably a corruption of 'conquerors'.

Having crossed the stile, you find, in three or four yards, another on your left. Negotiate this, pass another National Trust sign and enter Hanbury Park seeing, on the horizon ahead, the tower of Hanbury Church. After about 30 yards, the red-brick Hall comes into view, just visible amongst the surrounding trees. Just to the right of the Hall, in the near distance, is a single oak. This is the line of your path and, passing the oak and maintaining the same heading, you get good views of Hanbury Hall and its gardens, surrounded by a ha-ha, on your left. Passing over a stile, cross the main driveway with the wrought-iron main gates on your left.

The red-brick Hanbury Hall was built in 1701 by Thomas Vernon (1654-1721). Outstanding features are the painted ceilings and staircase by Sir James Thornhill and fine collections of eighteenth century English furniture and porcelain.

Moving on from the iron gates, pass the end of a line of lime trees and soon cross another stile. Continue on your way, aiming a little left of the church tower in the distance, passing a pool surrounded by trees on your left. Crossing a service drive and passing a small wired-off area, soon walk through a guard-of-honour of oaks of widely-differing ages, halfway along which you cross a stile.

On emerging from this avenue, cross a stile by a muddy gateway and then take a conspicuous path across the grassland and up the incline towards the church. When you reach the kissing gate at the top, you may need to regain your breath so you should turn round and enjoy your last view across the typical English countryside with the Malverns, on clear days, providing a dramatic backcloth. Passing through the gate, turn right and, in a few yards, right again to walk down the lane to your car. Or, if you are using public transport, continue reading from the start of the text.

If you are in need of refreshment continue along the road past the school for about half a mile to reach the Jinney Ring Craft Centre where there is a pleasant licensed restaurant (not open on Mondays). For details telephone 01527-821272.

14

A Circular Walk from Studley

This walk, starting in the small, but busy, town of Studley, leads through pleasant countryside and visits the ancient church of Morton Bagot, passes the impressive Studley Castle and reaches the somewhat isolated, but very attractive, Studley church.

Parking: Though there is some road-side parking in Studley, a free car park may be reached by taking the B4092 from the roundabout by the Barley Mow. After about half a mile, turn left into Crooks Lane and left again into Pool Road (GR072638). Leave the car park eastwards via a path to the right-hand side of Studley Infants' School. 200 yards on, the main A435 road is reached via Needle Close.
Maps: Landranger 150; Pathfinder 975.
Public Transport: Midland Red West service 146 (Birmingham – Evesham) stops in Alcester Road (A435), Studley, 300 yards south of the Barley Mow roundabout.
Start/Finish: Castle Road, Studley (GR073638).
Refreshments: The Swan, the Barley Mow and the Duke of Marlborough, all in Studley.
Distance: 7 miles.

THE walk begins on Castle Road which is opposite the War Memorial on the A435 and is just south of the bus stops and Needle Close. Walk down Castle Road for 200 yards and, opposite Bell Lane, turn right between houses into Gunners Lane and walk on for 200 yards. Take the second turn on the left into Mallard Road and then right into Wickham Road at the end of which cross a stile.

A clear path goes a little to the left across a sheep field with the River Arrow to the left. Cross a footbridge and, 50 yards beyond it, go through a kissing gate and turn right into a lane. Follow this as it swings left and passes a cemetery. At the end of the cemetery railings, turn sharp right and follow the boundary for about 300 yards.

When the hedge turns right, you continue slightly to the left of the original line aiming for the right margin of a tree-fringed pool. Passing this, veer a little to the left towards a large gap in the hedge ahead, having

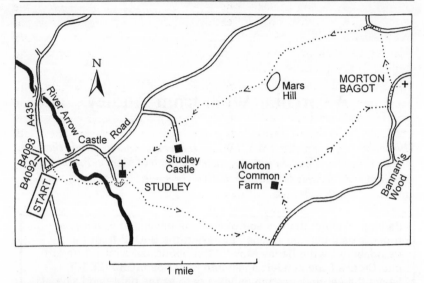

1 mile

passed through which, turn right onto a tractor track. This meanders alongside a stream and later swings right to cross the stream by a concrete bridge.

50 yards beyond the bridge, pass through a gate and immediately veer left, again to follow the stream, passing the earthworks of an ancient Priory on your right. Moving through a hedge gap at the end of the field, aim to the left of an electricity pylon to reach a metal farm gate. Go through the gate and turn right over a stream to follow the hedge boundary.

You are now entering pheasant country. At certain seasons of the year, there are scores of them feeding in the fields adjacent to the woodlands in which they are reared. Introduced, probably in Roman times from central and eastern Europe, the pheasant would surely have long-since disappeared had it not been for the protection afforded by the Game Laws and by gamekeepers.

At the field's end, a footbridge and a short detour to the right lead to a lane into which you turn left. After swinging right, and about 50 yards after passing the driveway to Morton Common Farm, take another driveway (waymarked) to the left which runs behind Morton Common Farm.

Just before the rear gate of the farm, climb a stile on the right in the shadow of an electricity post which bears a large transformer. There is a carefully-painted sign here which proclaims a 'Public Footpath to Church'. Go slightly left across this large field and climb another (crude) stile in the far left-hand corner. (Take care here – there is another stile on the left side of the field, but you want the one in the corner.) Walk ahead, with the field margin at your left hand. Reaching a hedge, climb a gate (serving as a crude stile) and go forward, still with a hedge on your left. Cross another insecure stile and walk onwards, now with a wire fence on your left and telegraph posts on your right.

At the end of this field pass through the second of two metal gates and, in less than 10 yards, take a similar gate to the right. Making a bee-line (ENE) for the red tiled tower of Morton Bagot Church (which is a few hundred yards ahead), in 40 yards pass though a metal gate and then walk on to the top of the next field. When you reach the hedge turn left and walk on past the end of a hedge which partially divides the field. After about a hundred yards look out for a stile on the right, this being easily missed as it is partly obscured by the hedge. Cross this awkward stile and walk up a slight incline with the hedge on the left and, particularly in the autumn, pleasant views ahead of Bannam's Wood. On reaching a lane, turn left and walk on to where a farm drive on the right leads to the tiny church of Morton Bagot.

Morton Bagot church

As is the case with so many such buildings in the country, vandalism and theft have required that this church remains locked except for services. However, peep through its clear-glass windows to see beautifully-embroidered kneelers, well-carved, wooden choir stalls, altar rail and furniture in the chancel and an east window dedicated to three members of the Peshall family who were, for long spells during the period 1820 to 1933, rectors of the parish.

Retreating back out of the churchyard and down the farm drive, cross the lane to a stile directly opposite. Climb this and walk ahead to reach a footbridge. If the footpath ahead is not visible walk up the field bearing slightly left and, when it comes into view, aim for a telegraph post 100 yards to the left of the white-painted houses. Cross a stile here and turn left into a narrow lane.

Passing a pool and noticing the ornately-carved barge boards of Morton Bagot Manor, soon turn left into a waymarked Private Road. You use a gate and two subsequent stiles to pass through the farmyard of Manor Farm, being warned by signs and noisy, tethered dogs to keep to the paths! After the second stile, pass down a field bearing slightly right to cross two more stiles separated by a gravel drive. Turn left and walk alongside a wire fence until, just beyond the lake, you climb a stile on the left and immediately turn right to walk along the field margin.

At the bottom of this field cross a stile to pass between twin, wire fences along a short narrow strip of land. Ignore the first stile (on the left) and then climb over the second which is preceded by a small concrete bridge. Now aim half-left for the space between the second and third of a line of oak trees which stand in the field. Beyond the trees, in the corner of the field, climb over a crude double fence stile, turn left and follow the tall hedge until, in the corner of the field, metal hurdles have to be climbed.

Walk straight ahead, up the right-hand boundary of the wooded Mars Hill, your direction being indicated for the next half-mile or so, by electricity wires. Descending the other side of the hill, you reach a rough stile surrounded by a variety of cattle-watering devices. Still following the wires, cross a field and pass through a gateway and, when the wires swing to the right, join a gravel-surfaced farm track which, after 100 yards or so, turns right.

In a further 25 yards, turn left over a stile again to follow the electricity poles to a gateway through which you pass and turn left. Finally leaving the cables behind, walk down a lane which wanders between houses, past the premises of a market-gardener towards Studley Castle. Your path crosses the main drive to the Castle which housed, at one time, an Agricultural College but is now used by the marketing division of a motor company. Undeterred by a metal barrier, continue ahead to reach a stile which gives access to a clear path leading back to Studley Church. At the near corner of the churchyard, a path leads across to the south door of the church.

The 700-year-old church of The Nativity of the Blessed Virgin Mary has many interesting features which include a carved, stone coffin lid in the chancel, a fine Norman doorway (only visible form the outside) and Norman window on the north wall and, adjacent to the pulpit, a carved Paschal Lamb thought to have some connections with the Knights Templar (to whom reference is made on Walk 6).

Leaving the churchyard by its main gate, turn left to the kissing gate through which you came earlier in the day. Cross the footbridge ahead and walk back along the river to reach a stile by the nearest house. Walk a few yards down the road, turn left into Mallard Road, then right into Gunners Lane and, in 200 yards, reach Castle Road into which you turn left to return to your starting point.

15

A Figure-of-Eight from
Wootton Wawen

Another contrasted walk which starts at the superb church at Wootton Wawen and uses a canal towpath and paths through fields and woodland with an optional diversion to cross the interesting Bearley Aqueduct.

Parking: The A3400 is unsuitable for parking but space should be found on road sides on the B4089 (to Alcester) (GR151632) and in Pettiford Lane (mentioned later) (GR159632).
Maps: Landranger 151; Pathfinder 975.
Public Transport: Stratford Blue service X20 (Birmingham – Stratford); British Rail: Birmingham to Stratford line (request stop at Wootton Wawen). From the railway station walk east to reach the Bull's Head, then turn right to reach the start of your walk at St Peter's Church.
Start/Finish: St Peter's Church, Wootton Wawen (GR153633).
Refreshments: The Bull's Head Inn and The Navigation Inn in Wootton Wawen.
Distance: 6½ miles (5 miles without the diversion to Bearley Aqueduct).

THE village is dominated by the superb St Peter's Church standing in a well-kept churchyard colourfully stocked, in the summer, with annual plants. A visit to this ancient church is strongly recommended, either at the start or the end of this walk.

According to the admirable guide book on sale within, St Peter's is 'one of the oldest, largest and structurally most noteworthy churches in Warwickshire'. It had its origins in the eighth century but the present building grew from a small Anglo-Saxon structure built c.1035-40. That building has, over intervening years, been much enlarged and modified into the architectural gem which we see today. As the incomparable Arthur Mee put it, with such prescience in the 1930s, 'The twentieth century rushes by in its cars, but time stands still in the church where the past has a thousand symbols'.

On leaving the quaint antiquity of the church, walk back to the main Stratford Road, turn left and keep to the left hand pavement of this busy

thoroughfare. Pass Wootton Hall and the impressive weirs on the River
Alne, taking note from the milepost carved into the stone balustrades on
either side of the roadway in 1806 that it's only 100 miles to London! Pass
a converted mill and a brick-built chapel and, immediately after Yew Tree
Farm, leave the bustle of the main road and turn left into a lane, taking
care as it has no pavement. (This is Pettiford Lane mentioned earlier as a
possible parking spot.)

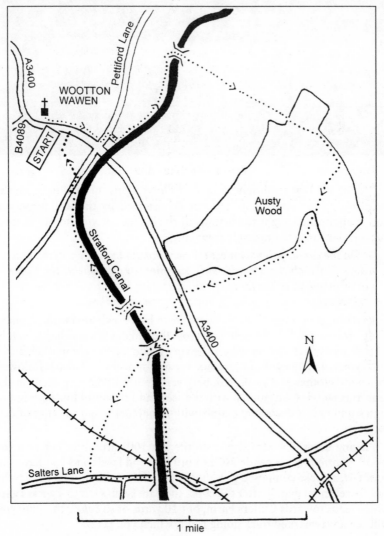

1 mile

Weirs on the River Alne

Taking the first turn right the path follows a private road to reach the Stratford-upon-Avon Canal. Do not be deterred by the well-preserved notice about the weight restrictions of the bridge for you do not cross it but turn left onto the nearside towpath.

> *On the canal, you may meet the occasional pleasure craft, the bow waves of which threaten, in early summer, to overwhelm the fluffy junior members of the family flotillas of local mallards – but they are very buoyant and, seemingly, always come up smiling!*

Pass bridge number 52 (which appears to lead nowhere) but, at the next bridge (number 51), turn right and cross the canal. On the other side, join a bridleway which can, in winter, be very muddy. After about a third of a mile, you reach Austy Wood, the north-east boundary of which is followed for about another 400 yards, climbing very gently all the way. Early in the year, this wood is sensational with the scent and colour of bluebells but in high summer it is decorated mainly with honeysuckle and varieties of dog rose.

Having ignored a wicket gate on the left 100 yards after entering the wood, continue your gentle ascent until the land levels and you have, on your left, a copse composed predominantly of silver birch. You need to be alert here! Immediately after the copse the path swings left to a wicket gate which leads towards Cutlers Farm, but 10 yards or so *before* this gate you will see a waymarked track going right, which you take.

You now meander through the privately-owned Austy Wood with occasional reassuring waymarks and taped-off areas. In summer you may hear the soft, purring call of the turtle dove. On reaching the edge of the wood, you are directed half right by a waymark and then keep to the southern boundary of developing woodland on a well-defined path with good views to the left over Warwickshire's well-wooded countryside. When the edge of the wood bends to the right the waymarked path takes you forward across the field and then through a strip of woodland to reach the Stratford Road.

We need to cross this but please bear in mind the danger here for this straight road does invite some motorists to drive as Jehu the son of Nimshi was supposed to have done. (One translation of 2 Kings Ch. IX, verse 20 reports that 'he drove like a madman' – in his chariot, of course!)

Having crossed the road, turn left and use the rudimentary asphalt pavement. Ignore the first right turn (to Hill Farm) but take the second (waymarked) track, which occurs just before the main road swings to the left. Cross a cattle grid and, following this rough, gravelly lane, reach a canal bridge.

(Just before the bridge – number 56 – is a stile and wooden staircase on the right which give access to the nearside towpath. This should be used by those who are taking the shorter walk. If you wish to do this, walk with the canal on your left and continue reading from ✳ on page 66.)

Continuing the longer walk, cross the canal, take a waymarked stile on the left just before the gates of Sillesbourne Rise and immediately turn right and follow the field boundary. After about 100 yards, cross a stile and turn left. Keeping on the same bearing, keep a hedge on your left and cross two stiles. The hedge now becomes rather intermittent but continue with this still on your left until having crossed another two stiles, you come to the railway line. Cross the line with care and, having done this, walk across the pasture ahead towards a metal footbridge. Having crossed this, go left and, very soon, right across a disused railway track.

Make for a stile directly across the field, climb over it and turn left into Salters Lane on the far side of which is a fairly wide grass verge to keep you off the tarmac. Ahead you soon see the Bearley Aqueduct which carries the Stratford-upon-Avon Canal across the road and the adjacent railway lines. Go under the aqueduct and immediately turn right and climb steps up to the towpath.

Bearley Aqueduct, over 150 yards long and supported by thirteen brick piers, is of a sturdy cast-iron construction which has stood the test of time. Its towpath is level with the canal bed so you have an unusual view of passing craft! Although, unlike its little brother that you may have seen earlier at Wootton Wawen, it bears no plaque commemorating its completion in 1813, it is a fitting memorial to those Victorian engineers who designed and built such structures.

Having reached the towpath, turn right and walk across the aqueduct and, passing Bearley Lock No. 39, reach bridge 56 so completing the loop and rejoining the shorter route.

✶ *Continue from here on the shorter walk.*

Cross the next bridge (number 55) and use the towpath on the west side to follow the canal back towards Wootton Wawen. At the next bridge (number 54), turn to the left and walk down a rough lane to reach a metalled road into which you turn right.

After about 50 yards, pass through a waymarked (rather rickety) gate on the left and go half right through a spinney to a stile. Having negotiated this, aim a little right of the church tower to a rough vehicle track onto which you turn right and walk past a pair of impressive stone eagles to the main road to return to your transport in the village.

16

Feckenham – and its Friendly Fuel

Starting in the pleasant village of Feckenham, this walk explores the adjacent countryside and, after walking down the sombrely-named Burial Lane, leads back to the village and its interesting church. For those who depend on public transport, this walk can be combined with Walk 17 which starts at Astwood Bank.

Parking: There is a free car park in Feckenham on the west side of High Street about 100 yards from the B4090 (GR 009615).
Maps: Landranger 150; Pathfinder 975.
Public Transport: No convenient service to Feckenham. However, by combining this walk with Walk 17 you can use the Midland Red West service 70 from Redditch to Astwood Bank.
Start/Finish: Feckenham High Street (GR009615).
Refreshments: The Lygon Arms (on the B4090 at its intersection with High Street) and the Rose and Crown (on High Street), both in Feckenham.
Distance: 4 miles.
Extended Walk: This walk can be combined with Walk 17 to give a combined distance of 9 miles.

ON leaving the car park, turn left into High Street and follow this for 50 yards to reach The Green. On the opposite side of this and a little to the left, by the side of 'The Old Vicarage', you will see the church driveway which you enter. You can visit the church later so, about 15 yards after passing through its main gates, fork right across the churchyard towards an isolated, metal kissing gate and then walk ahead, leaving the church on your left, through a metal wicket gate in a red-brick wall.

This leads to a gravel path which ends, in about a hundred yards, at another metal kissing gate. Having passed through this and its twin on the opposite side of a driveway, turn sharp left. After keeping the boundaries of two fields on your left, veer a few yards to the right to reach a footbridge (somewhat obscured by a bush) which you cross. Turn right into a large meadow and walk, with the stream not far from your right hand, to a stile directly ahead at the opposite side of this grassland, 40 yards to the left of a red-brick house. Crossing the stile you will enter an area which is planted with rows of willows, an unusual crop!

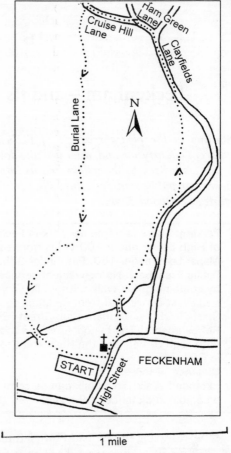

These willows will never feel the effect of the leather of a cricket ball – they are destined to be burned. After five or six years' rapid growth, they will be felled, broken into chips and fed into modern, heat-efficient stoves. A cheap fuel indeed and one against which the term 'pollution' cannot be levelled. Yes, when burned they produce the dreaded 'greenhouse gas', carbon dioxide, which provides the blanket for global warming, but they are just giving back that which they took in during their recent growth. The books are balanced – albeit the debt is repaid five or six years late, but better than the ancient debts paid when burning fossil fuels such as coal or gas!

Go straight ahead and, at the end of the willow field, you have to move a little to the left to find the stile but, having crossed it, resume your stream-side path, passing venerable old willows of the wild variety. When you leave the field, via a stile which is preceded by a deep ditch, beyond you will see two mature oaks which stand in line ahead in the field about 50 yards to the left of the stream. Reaching the second of these, bear left, passing an even older oak which is part of an intermittent hedge and keep on that same heading to a stile 100 yards ahead.

Beyond that stile, continue straight up an incline to pass through a metal gate (adjacent to a cattle trough). From here, swing slightly left in the direction of the top right-hand corner of the field where you pass through another metal gate to reach Clayfields Lane into which you turn left to walk up to Ham Green. On reaching a T-junction, turn left into Ham Green Lane and soon take another left turn into Cruise Hill Lane which you follow, having passed several attractively-maintained, timber-framed houses. At the top of the lane, you may pause at the farm gate which faces you.

You are confronted with a splendid view across Worcestershire with the Malverns prominent to the south-west and Droitwich, with its tall, dark water tower, due west. Before you leave, you may notice, immediately behind you, a disused chapel, heavily-overgrown and, as the estate agents might say, 'ripe for development'.

From Cruise Hill, take the sign-posted Burial Lane down which funeral corteges passed in by-gone days. After about a hundred yards, pass through a wicket gate onto a bridle path which, during winter, may be very muddy. Then follow this gently-descending, well-defined path, ignoring stiles at its side and making use of its many horse-hoofmarks which act as unofficial waymarks!

About two hundred yards beyond a large electricity pylon pass though a metal wicket gate, soon to reach a long, narrow strip of grassland. You might well hear across the meadows, on the hour and the half hour, the church clock announcing the passage of time. About 120 yards after this strip of grassland ends, you will see a metal sign-post which indicates that you should take a left turn, using a bridleway to 'The Square'.

About a hundred yards down this path cross a substantial footbridge, with a waterfall on the left, and swing left to pass between a pool and a tall cupressus hedge, then bypassing a redundant footbridge beside a former mill (The Old Mill House). Soon bear slightly left into a gravel lane which becomes tarmacked and passes the Feckenham Cricket Club ground on the left. You soon reach the Village Green just before the end of which you will see, on your left, the path which you used earler leading to the Church.

The squat-towered Parish Church is dedicated to Saint John the Baptist. Near the pulpit is a list of vicars of the parish, Thomas de Northleach being the first, in 1235, and it was during his incumbency that the fine pointed arches on round pillars on the north side of the nave were built. Over the south door, one of the Charity Boards commemorates gifts of between £1 and £30 from five parishioners in 1765, these sums to be invested 'and such interest to be desposed of by the Minister for the time being for ever to such Poor People of this Parish as he should think deserving of such charity'.

On leaving the Church, retreat down the driveway and rejoin High Street to find the car park 50 yards along on the right.

17

Astwood Bank and Feckenham

Leading from the busy Evesham Road in Astwood Bank this walk crosses nearby farmland to and from Feckenham and thus readily links with Walk 16.

Parking: Roadside in Gorsey Close, Astwood Bank (GR041620). (From the Evesham Road towards the south end of the village, turn into Avenue Road which is beside the Bell Inn. Continue down Avenue Road from which Gorsey Close leads off to the left after about 300 yards.)
Map: Landranger 150; Pathfinder 975.
Public Transport: Midland Red West service 70 (Redditch – Astwood Bank). Alight in Avenue Road and walk back along Avenue Road until it swings off to the right opposite Gorsey Close.
Start/Finish: Avenue Road, Astwood Bank (GR041620).
Refreshments: In Feckenham, the Lygon Arms (on the B4090 at its intersection with High Street) and the Rose and Crown (on High Street). In Astwood Bank, the Bell Inn and the White Lion.
Distance: 5 miles.
Extended Walk: This walk can be combined with Walk 16 (which starts from Feckenham) to give a combined distance of 9 miles.

ALONGSIDE No. 75 Avenue Road, at the intersection of that road and Gorsey Close is Doe Bank Drive. Walk down this tarmacked lane for about 200 yards and, when it veers sharply to the right to Doe Bank House, find a green gate on your left with a stile beside it. Having crossed the stile, walk on an enclosed bridleway for 50 yards and then pass through a gate to enter a field.

You are now on the Monarch's Way, a long-distance path which links Worcester with Charmouth on the south coast. Having ignored the stile on your left soon after entering the field, enjoy good views ahead of the Worcestershire countryside as you walk onwards, with the hedge on your left-hand side, to cross another stile.

Keeping on the same heading, you gradually descend towards the large buildings of Astwood Farm. Pass through two gateways to the right of

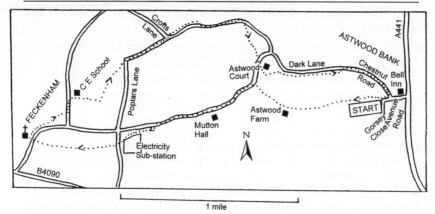

1 mile

these buildings and, at green silos, bear right onto a concrete drive. Passing the black-and-white farmhouse and a modern bungalow, continue down this conifer-lined drive until you reach its iron gates.

Pass through these to reach a road (Astwood Lane) into which you turn left, initially using the wide grass verge on your nearside. After about 300 yards, the road narrows significantly, requiring extra attention and single-file walking on its right-hand side as it passes Mutton Hall. Just beyond this farm, wider verges reappear. After about 500 yards and several twists and turns of the road, look out on the left for an easily missed finger-post ('Public Footpath Feckenham') and stile directing you onto a path between the road and a prominent earth-bank.

After a further 100 yards, pass through a wooden gate and turn left to walk up a roadway towards an electricity sub-station. Just before metal railings, turn right up a short flight of brick steps and follow the sign-posted footpath towards Feckenham, keeping an old hawthorn hedge and the railings on your left.

Cross a lane via two stiles and then, keeping to its left-hand hedge, walk up a field towards a stile which is adjacent to a cattle-trough – this making the area very wet in winter. (If the morass is impenetrable, a gap in the hedge 30 yards to the right may provide an escape route!)

Having negotiated this stile, proceed up the incline, aiming 20 yards to the right of a well-proportioned horse chestnut tree on the immediate horizon. Do not be lured towards an attractive, wooden kissing gate in the far left-hand corner, but make for a gateway midway along the facing hedge. Pass through this and walk on with the hedge on your right. About 20 yards from the end of the field, cross a stile and continue with the hedge now on your other side and the tower of Feckenham church ahead of you. The hedge gives way to a red-brick wall beside which you walk to reach High Street. Here turn left and walk 50 yards to The Green and, maybe, pause in this pleasant spot. From The Green, a prominent driveway on the right leads to the church.

Fuller notes on the ancient Parish Church of Saint John the Baptist are given on Walk 16. You may well wish to go in and look at yet another fine example of our rich heritage of English country churches.

If you are combining this walk with Walk 16 this is the point to change over.

On leaving the church turn left to pass a waymarked kissing gate which stands isolated amongst the weathered, leaning gravestones and then swing left to reach a metal wicket-gate at the left-hand end of another red-brick wall. Pass through this to walk along a gravel path. By way of a pair of metal kissing gates, cross a driveway and continue across the field on a well-trodden path to the car park of a well-known leisure outfitters' premises.

Continue to the far left corner of this car park to find a narrow path which, in 10 yards, leads to another kissing gate and a concrete footbridge. Cross this and turn right to use an asphalt path towards a gate which gives access to a lane (Swansbrook Lane). Here turn left and use the pavement to walk to the brow of a short incline where you turn right and walk along a lane in front of Feckenham Church of England School.

At the end of the lane, cross a waymarked stile walking straight ahead with the hedge on your left, ignoring the stile on the immediate left. After about 100 yards, the field continues as a narrow channel just before the end of which you take a stile to the left and walk up a slope with the hedge to your right.

At the top of the incline, cross another stile and walk on, with the hedge still on your right, to meet a stile beside a metal gate. Cross this and aim diagonally down a slope to a stile in the far corner of the field. Cross this stile and turn left to join the rough-surfaced Poplars Lane, following this as it swings right and gently rises. Where Poplars Lane joins the tarmacked Crofts Lane, cross the stile opposite and walk ahead with the hedge on your right accompanied, in springtime, by gambolling lambs.

Some 200 yards before the extensive buildings of Astwood Hill Farm, ignore the waymarks ahead and pass through the farm gate on your right. Re-joining Crofts Lane, turn left and walk on, past stables and, about 100 yards past the last house ('Green Acres'), find an easily missed plank bridge and stile on the right. Cross these, traverse a small paddock to cross another stile, and then continue, more-or-less on the same heading, to another plank bridge and waymarked stile under an oak tree. Climb over this and then veer slightly right to another stile over paddock railings. You are now back on the Monarch's Way. Pass through a plantation of young hardwood trees, to another stile. Leaving the Monarch's Way, aim for a stile (not the metal gate) in the hedge 60 yards ahead.

Climb over this, cross the road (Astwood Lane again) and use a plank bridge just to the right of a red-brick wall. Over the bridge, cross a double stile through a line of evergreens and walk on with the boundary of a large complex of renovated buildings on your left. Keeping to the left-hand margin of the field, you now walk ahead beside Dark Lane which is some feet below you, behind hedges on your left. The path, which soon becomes enclosed, crosses several stiles and the driveways of Blackthorn House and of a water company before it enters a field.

If you have followed this walk in springtime, you will have noticed how common is the blackthorn in this area and how appropriate is the name Blackthorn House! This tree, with its black bark and long, sharp thorns, especially in late, cold springs produces its abundant white flowers before its leaves emerge, thus providing impressive drifts of white in the leafless hedgerows. This is the tree which provides the

Approaching Feckenham

sloes with which sloe gin can be made and the wood from which the Irishman's shillelagh can be fashioned!

Following the left-hand margin of the field up an incline, you finally have no choice but to descend into Dark Lane via a sloping path and steep steps. Turn right into the lane and follow it as it ascends sharply and continue ahead into Chestnut Road. The bus stop is on the left past Chapel Lane: if you have left your car in Gorsey Close continue to the T-junction where Chestnut Road meets Avenue Road and turn right.

18

Round About Coughton Court

A pleasant stroll, on level ground, with the River Arrow always close at hand and with the option of visiting the imposing Coughton Court.

Parking: There is ample road-side parking in Coughton Fields Lane which runs west from the A435 Birmingham to Evesham road from GR081603.

Maps: Landranger 150; Pathfinder 975.

Public Transport: Midland Red West service 146 (Birmingham – Evesham) stops at Coughton Fields Lane.

Start/Finish: Coughton (GR081603).

Refreshments: Throckmorton Arms (on A435) and at Coughton Court.

Distance: 3½ miles.

Special Feature: Coughton Court (National Trust). It is open to the public and opening times may be checked by telephoning 01789-400777.

WALK down Coughton Fields Lane to reach a pretty ford over the River Arrow. On a sunny, summer afternoon, this is a pleasant place to watch paddling children and to feed dabbling ducks. Cross the footbridge and, as soon as you reach the end of the descending path on the far side, turn sharply to the left, cross the lane and pass through a five-barred gate which is followed immediately by a metal one with side wicket. Walk through this and proceed along a farm track for about 50 yards at which point swing left onto a green track which works back towards trees which border the Arrow. In summer, the smell of wild garlic is pervasive here.

The wild garlic or, to give it another name, ramsons is mentioned commonly in books, both old and new, which deal with edible and medicinal plants. Being rich in vitamin C, its young leaves are said to be useful in salads. Some authors claim that the plant offers an effective treatment for a number of human ailments. However, this being merely a walks book, provision of further details would be unwise!

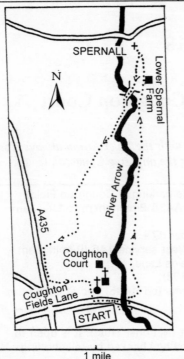

Cross a stile by a metal farm gate and, bearing slightly right to keep to the edge of oak-studded parkland, you have the lush green flood plain on your left, beyond which you gain good views of the gardens and rear façade of Coughton Court. Proceeding in the same direction, pass through a gate mid-way in a field boundary which links two mature woodland copses.

Maintain this heading across the next field and over a sturdy wooden foot-bridge. You will now see, ahead of you, a red-brick farm (Lower Spernall Farm): aim for the electricity pylon to its left. At the next field boundary, veer a little to the left, aiming at the second pylon to the left of the farm. By the time you reach the next boundary, having in mid-summer had the benefit of free weather commentaries from the abundant scarlet pimpernel alias Poor-Man's-Weatherglass, the farm is near.

Proceeding through a gate, walk towards the right-hand edge of the trees which you can see immediately ahead. These conceal the Arrow and, if you approach fairly quietly, you may well disturb a heron from its angling business. Walking close to the river, come to a stile from which you proceed straight across meadowland aiming slightly to the right of a small church adjacent to a house. (At this point note, on your left, a metal footbridge which you will use on your return journey.) In the autumn this meadow sports fairy rings and other fungi, some edible – but others certainly not!

The former Church of St. Leonard's, Spernall probably had its origins in the twelfth century. It is now closed for worship (and to casual visitors!) but is preserved by The Ancient Monuments Society. This is a quiet place for pause and meditation.

Leaving the old church, retrace your steps across the meadow to the footbridge and cross it. The path meanders back downstream for the first couple of furlongs, the Arrow never being far away on your left. The field

Spernall Church

tapers and, at its end, cross a double stile with Coughton Court clearly visible across the grassland straight ahead. Don't go directly towards the Court, but aim about 30° to its right, passing towards the far right-hand corner of a sheep pasture. There pass through a metal gate in the shade of an oak. Go forward, bearing slightly right towards the hedge which accommodates some more splendid oaks, one of which must be the best part of 300 years old. If only it could tell its tale!

At this field's end, you find a stile on your right hand. Cross this and move ahead to another stile. Having crossed this, aim slightly left towards a house, passing rookeries to left and right, to reach the busy A435. Turn left and use the pavement to continue your walk southwards, in the direction of Alcester. You soon see the handsome frontage of Coughton Court on your left. Sadly, the Dutch Disease has deprived it of its fine avenue of elms but it remains an imposing sight. Ignore all beckoning entrances until you meet a white, metal kissing gate through which you pass to walk along a grassy path towards the fine building ahead.

The construction of Coughton Court that we see today was begun early in the sixteenth century by Sir George Throckmorton, though the estate had been owned by the family since 1409. Its fine Tudor gatehouse is one of its noteworthy features. The Court is now owned by the National Trust.

Having visited the Court you may also wish to examine the adjacent church.

The church of St Peter is a fine, light building, parts of which date from the early sixteenth century. The remains of many members of the Throckmorton family rest here in ornate tombs. There is also ancient stained glass, a peal of six bells which dates from 1686 and a clock, made by a local blacksmith in 1690 and still keeping perfect time, which strikes the hours loudly but has no faces or hands – songs without words indeed!

Leaving the churchyard, turn left onto a driveway leading away from the Court. Near the end of this pass a Roman Catholic church, built in 1857, a few yards beyond which you reach Coughton Fields Lane where you find your car or turn right to use public transport on the A435.

19

The Shakespeare Connection

A delightful rural walk, starting at Aston Cantlow, crossing the River Alne twice, passing through quiet countryside and visiting a youthful-looking centenarian.

Parking: Car park behind the King's Head at Aston Cantlow (GR138599), but please ask the publican's permission first. Otherwise roadside parking.
Maps: Landranger 150/151; Pathfinder 975 and 997.
Public Transport: Stagecoach service 228 (Stratford-upon-Avon – Redditch) stops at Aston Cantlow (limited service).
Start/Finish: The King's Head, Aston Cantlow (GR138599).
Refreshments: The King's Head at Aston Cantlow.
Distance: 4 miles.

L EAVING the King's Head, walk down Church Lane to the main street. Here turn left and walk through the village. Turn left into Chapel Lane and, when this swings abruptly to the right, continue on for about 60 yards to cross a stile. Proceeding on the same heading, you soon reach a pair of stiles by which you cross a clearly-defined, disused railway track. You will then see, 150 yards or so across the field and slightly to the right, a metal footbridge in a clump of trees.

Use the bridge to cross the River Alne and the line of the bridge points you in exactly the direction you need to follow in the next field, up a slope towards a dip on the horizon. At the top of the field, cross the road to a stile on the opposite side. Going over this, walk straight across the field at 90° to the line of the fence behind you, aiming for a gap in the hedge ahead. Go through this gap and turn left onto a grassy bridleway with the hedge and a stream now on your left. The surface changes to a cinder track for a short distance but you stay on this heading for nearly a mile.

Just after the cinder path veers off to the right, you pass a line of aspen trees. The leaves of aspen, with their pale green undersides, are attached by slender stalks. This results in their being agitated by the slightest breeze and explains the Latin name, Populus tremula.

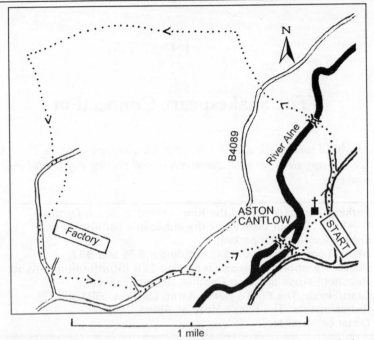

About two-thirds of the way up the gentle incline, cross a stile beside two metal gates and resume your former direction with the hedge now on your right. Ignoring a plank bridge and stile on your right in about 150 yards, continue to the top of the slope where you leave the bridleway which swings off to the right. At this point, you turn left to follow a track with the hedge to your right.

Bearing a little to the right at a barn and with horse paddocks to the left, you reach and cross a stile which is under a curved oak tree on the right hand side. After about 100 yards, you cross another stile on your left and continue in the same direction but with the hedge now on your right! You now walk down a slope to a lane into which you turn left.

Walk up the lane and turn right immediately before the buildings of Hill Farm. Walk ahead for about 100 yards to pass a redundant stile at the end of a holly hedge. Here, bear slightly right walking to the far right hand corner of the field where you see, at the bottom of a slope, a stile. Cross this and follow a very rough path through mixed woodland which skirts factory premises. Emerge from the woodland via a stile into a lane where you turn left and walk ahead towards Great Alne.

On a grassy triangle at a road intersection in about 500 yards, you will see an oak tree planted in 1887 to mark the Jubilee of Queen Victoria. Here's a centenarian! Noting that its trunk diameter is about

30 inches, it may help you to estimate the age of some of the giant old oaks referred to elsewhere in this book!

Continuing past the intersection, just beyond the drive of Fir Croft, take a path to your left which runs for a distance of about 500 yards through a narrow strip of woodland (ignoring a branch off to the right). During their nesting season, the inhabitants of a rookery here have much to say to one another!

Soon after passing Great Alne Cricket Club's ground, cross the factory drive by a black-and-white house to reach a road. Turn left into the B4089 and, using its ample grass verge, walk on for about 350 yards to where it swings abruptly to the left. Here you take a rough lane on the right and, 20 yards past the gateway of an electricity sub-station, turn left to follow a waymarked path, with the hum of the sub-station on your left.

At a sad-looking, stone-built bridge over the disused railway you swing slightly left and cross a stile. Turning left, walk along the edge of the disused track – the same one that you crossed earlier but, here, much more overgrown. After about 150 yards, swing to your right towards a footbridge between two stiles adjacent to a caravan park. The path continues straight ahead, the River Alne now separating you from the caravans.

At a sharp bend of the river, the path swings right to a footbridge. Pass over this, walk onwards over a gravel lane and then straight ahead between caravans to another footbridge by a rushing weir. Pass over this and through the wicket gate at its end to reach a road into which you turn left. After about 30 yards, pass through a wicket gate on the left onto a clear path which leads you past the Old School House to Aston Cantlow Church.

The seat in the churchyard of the peaceful Parish Church of St. John the Baptist might be a suitable spot for rest and contemplation but you should not leave without, if it is unlocked, looking inside this lovely building.

The Domesday Book of 1086 mentions a priest at Aston Cantlow, so you have here a fine example of ancient (and more modern) architecture. There are many gems within, adequately described on guide-cards. However, perhaps the church's most popular claim to fame is that John Shakespeare and Mary Arden, parents of the famous William, were very probably married here.

Leaving the churchyard via its lychgate you will see the entrance to the King's Head car park opposite.

20

A Ramble from Mary Arden's House

This short walk is designed to augment a visit to Mary Arden's House and it takes in the towpath of the nearby Stratford Canal and public footpaths through neighbouring sheep pastures.

Parking: There is free parking at Mary Arden's House at Wilmcote (GR165582) for visitors so, if you intend to tour the house, this will be the place to park. However, make sure that you note the times at which the gates are locked! Otherwise roadside parking.
Maps: Landranger 151; Pathfinder 997.
Public Transport: Trains on the Birmingham – Stratford-upon-Avon line, and Stagecoach bus service 228 (Stratford-upon-Avon – Redditch; limited service) stop at Wilmcote.
Start/Finish: Wilmcote (GR165582).
Refreshments: Mary Arden's House, Mary Arden Inn and the Mason's Arms in Wilmcote.
Distance: 2½ miles.
Special Feature: Mary Arden's House. Opening times may be checked by telephoning 01789-293455.

ASSUMING that you will tour Mary Arden's House at the end of the walk, leave the car park and turn left into Station Road. Immediately after crossing the canal bridge, turn left to reach the towpath of the Stratford-upon-Avon Canal . Walking northwards (i.e. away from the bridge) for 250 yards, you find, just beyond a winding hole (where the canal widens to allow boats to turn), a metal wicket gate on your right.

Go through this, climb brick steps and use a path which passes through a patch of rough woodland and crosses a private drive soon to reach a railway line. Cross this with caution and walk along the path opposite for just over 100 yards.

You then cross a stile and, following the waymark, go half-right across the field to a plank bridge alongside a decrepit and redundant stile. Now going slightly to the right of your previous heading, cross a field towards a hedge. When you reach a farm lane in front of the hedge, turn sharp left

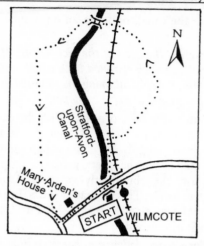

and follow the lane. This soon swings to the right thereafter being flanked by alternating varieties of poplar trees.

Just before a clump of trees which marks the site of the former Hardwick Farm, follow the lane as it swings left and leads back to the railway line. Using the railway company's advice, 'Stop. Look. Listen', you cross the double track.

After 30 yards or so, leave the rough track as it diverts left and go straight ahead onto a grassy path through

Mary Arden's House

scrubland. This soon leads back to the canal, opposite an un-numbered bridge.

As you cross the bridge, notice that the head of the arch is split. It was more expensive to build bridges which spanned both canal and towpath. This is the cheaper option, the split allowing the towrope to be passed through as the horse progressed along the towpath.

Having crossed the bridge, climb a stile and turn left. With the canal hidden on your left, you soon reach a barn which is associated with the now-derelict Broadlow Cottage. Swing slightly left and pass through a metal gate and cross the field to a stile by another metal gate. Do not pass over this, but turn left and follow the abundantly-waymarked path more-or-less southwards for over half a mile. This ultimately skirts the rear of Mary Arden's House, access to which is gained by turning left into Aston Cantlow Road and left again into Station Road.

The Tudor farmhouse in which Mary Arden, mother of William Shakespeare, grew up has an adjoining museum of farming and country life, daily falconry displays and other facilities. The open-topped coaches of the Guide Friday company call at the house on their guided tours from Stratford. For timetable details, phone 01789-294466.

Having savoured the magnificence of the house and its surroundings, your day's walk is complete.

Index

Also from Meridian...

HEART OF ENGLAND HILL WALKS
by John Newson

Eighteen circular walks exploring a variety of hills in the Heart of England – some well known, others that may be less familiar. The distances of the main walks vary from 10½ to 14½ miles. However, most include the option of a shorter walk and these range between 6 and 10 miles.

ISBN 1 869922 30 1. £5.95. 96 pages. 21 photographs. 18 maps. Paperback. A5.

THE MONARCH'S WAY
by Trevor Antill

A new long distance walk that closely follows the route taken by Charles II after his defeat by Cromwell's forces at Worcester in 1651. Visiting many historic places, perhaps previously known to readers only through the history books, it also goes through some of the finest scenery in western and southern England.

Book 1: Worcester to Stratford-upon-Avon. 175 miles.

ISBN 1 869922 27 1. £5.95. 112 pages. 19 photographs, 8 drawings, 19 maps. Paperback.

Book 2: Stratford-upon-Avon to Charmouth. 210 miles.

ISBN 1 869922 28 X. £6.95. 136 pages. 21 photographs. 23 maps. Paperback.

Book 3: Charmouth to Shoreham. 225 miles.

ISBN 1 869922 29 8. £6.95. 136 pages. 21 photographs. 25 maps. Paperback.

IN THE FOOTSTEPS OF THE GUNPOWDER PLOTTERS
by Conall Boyle

When the Gunpowder Plotters failed to blow up Parliament they fled, visiting their houses in Warwickshire and Worcestershire. In this unique guide you can follow their trail – by car, by bicycle, or on foot.

ISBN 1 869922 23 9. £4.95. 96 pages. 13 drawings. 19 maps. Paperback.

FAVOURITE WALKS IN THE WEST MIDLANDS
by members of the Birmingham CHA Rambling Club
Edited by Tom Birch and Mary Wall

A collection of twenty-two attractive walks from members of one of Birmingham's oldest walking clubs.

ISBN 1 869922 26 3. £4.95. 112 pages. 24 photographs. 23 maps. Paperback.

RIDGES and VALLEYS
Walks in the Midlands
by Trevor Antill

A selection of walks in the counties of Shropshire, Staffordshire and Worcestershire, taking in some of the better known, and some lesser known hills.

ISBN 1 869922 15 8. £3.95. 96 pages. 12 photographs. 19 maps. Paperback.

RIDGES and VALLEYS II
More Walks in the Midlands
by Trevor Antill

Following the theme established in the first volume, Trevor Antill describes eighteen further walks in Shropshire, Staffordshire and Worcestershire.

ISBN 1 869922 20 4. £4.95. 112 pages. 21 photographs. 19 maps. Paperback.

RIDGES and VALLEYS III
A Third Collection of Walks in the Midlands
by Trevor Antill

Readers of the previous two volumes will not be disappointed with this new collection of eighteen more Shropshire, Staffordshire and Worcestershire walks.

ISBN 1 869922 22 0. £4.95 112 pages. 11 photographs. 19 maps. Paperback.

THE NAVIGATION WAY: A Hundred Mile Towpath Walk
by Peter Groves and Trevor Antill

Starting from the centre of Birmingham and encompassing fourteen West Midlands canals the Navigation Way follows a meandering course through varied urban areas and delightful countryside.

ISBN 1 869922 19 0. £4.95. 112 pages. 31 photographs. 24 maps. Paperback.

HIDDEN HEREFORDSHIRE
A Book of Country Walks
by Julie Meech

Twenty circular walks in a beautiful county.

ISBN 1 869922 16 6. £4.95. 112 pages. 21 photographs. 20 maps. Paperback.

WATERSIDE WALKS in the MIDLANDS
by Birmingham Ramblers, edited by Peter Groves

Twenty-two walks featuring brooks, streams, pools, rivers and canals.

ISBN 1 869922 09 3. £4.95. 112 pages. 28 photographs. 22 maps. Paperback.

Prices correct December 1996

Available from booksellers or, if in difficulty, direct from Meridian Books. Please send remittance, adding the following amounts for postage and packing: order value up to £5.00 add 75p; up to £10.00 add £1.00; over £10.00 add £1.50.

Meridian Books
40 Hadzor Road • Oldbury • Warley • West Midlands • B68 9LA

Please write for our complete catalogue.